Nita Mehta's
TANDOORI
COOKING in the OVEN

Nita Mehta's
TANDOORI
COOKING in the OVEN

Nita Mehta

M.Sc. (Food & Nutrition), Gold Medalist

&

TANYA MEHTA

SNAB

Publishers Pvt. Ltd.

Nita Mehta's
TANDOORI
COOKING in the OVEN

© Copyright 2002 **SNAB** Publishers Pvt Ltd

First Hard Bound Edition 2002

ISBN 81-7869-033-0

Food Styling & Photography: **SNAB**

Layout and laser typesetting:

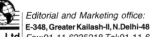

National Information
Technology Academy
3A/3, Asaf Ali Road
New Delhi-110002
☎ 3252948

Picture on cover:	Til Tikka, Burrah Kebab
	Ajwaini Machhi
Picture on page 1:	Mewa Seekh
	Tandoori Masala Pomfret
	Khumb Malai Tikka
Picture on page 2:	Akbari Kebabs
	Methi Machhi Tikka
Picture on last page:	Lamb Tikka Masala
	Achaari Paneer Tikka
Picture on back cover:	Malai Tikka

Published by:

SNAB
Publishers Pvt Ltd
3A/3 Asaf Ali Road
New Delhi-110002

The Best of Cookery Books

Editorial and Marketing office:
E-348, Greater Kailash-II, N.Delhi-48
Fax:91-11-6235218 Tel:91-11-6214011, 6238727
E-Mail: nitamehta@email.com
         snab@snabindia.com

Printed at:
THOMSON PRESS (INDIA) LIMITED

Distributed by:
THE VARIETY BOOK DEPOT
A.V.G. Bhavan, M 3 Con Circus
New Delhi - 110 001
Tel: 3327175, 3322567; Fax: 3714335

Price: Rs. 245/-

Introduction

Offer your loved ones tandoori food from your kitchen even if you do not have the conventional clay tandoor. Mouth watering tikkas and succulent kebabs can be on the table, fresh from the oven. No more buying ready made ones from the market! No more long hours in the kitchen too.

Tandoori food is amazingly quick and simple to prepare. So do not hesitate to try out these wonderful recipes. You will definitely be rewarded by the delightful results. A gas tandoor can also be used very successfully instead of the oven or the conventional clay tandoor. To give more value to the book, we have also included some delicious pan fried kebabs & seekhs in the book. Breads, chutneys and other accompaniments of a tandoori meal too are given to make the book complete.

Marination is an important part of tandoori cooking. All kebabs, tikkas etc. are marinated atleast ½ to 1 hour before being put in the oven. Marination is necessary for tenderizing the tough fibres of the meat and for the flavours to penetrate deeply into the meat or the vegetable. Tenderizers like raw papaya paste, kachri powder, lemon juice, tamarind pulp, soda-bi- carbonate play an important role. They are added to soften the mutton. A little cream/oil have been added to the marinades to prevent drying of the kebabs while grilling. Rich spices and flavourful seeds such as nutmeg (*jaiphal*), mace (*javetri*), sesame seeds (*til*), black cumin (*shah jeera*), cinnamon (*dalchini*), *green cardamom* (chhoti illaichi), *fennel*(saunf) and pistachio, almond and cashew pastes etc., have been used in the marinades to impart a subtle flavour to the tikkas and kebabs. Some rich tikkas/kebabs for parties or special occasions like *til tikka, mewa seekh, baadami tangri, burrah kebab, poodina kaju kebab, matar makhana kebab, tandoori masala pomfret* etc. are sure to be a hit at any party. Serve kebabs from this book as snacks or transform tikkas to masala dishes like meal time dishes — *lamb tikka masala, chicken tikka masala, tandoori paneer ki subzi* etc. Enjoy!!

Nita Mehta

Contents

FISH & SEA FOOD   64

VEGETARIAN   81

INDIAN BREADS

Paranthas, Nans & Rotis **108**

CHUTNEYS 116

ACCOMPANIMENTS 122

Important Tips...
Do go through these to get perfect results

- Grilling or roasting should be done on constant moderate heat, and not on very high heat. High heat toughens the proteins of the meat or paneer, making the kebabs shrink and turn hard.

- Always place the tikkas or the kebabs on the grill or on the wire rack and never directly on a tray. When you place them on a tray, the liquid that drips while grilling keeps collecting around the food and keeps the food wet all the time. This prevents the tandoori food from getting crisp on the outside. Whereas, if the food is placed on the wire rack, the liquid drips down and food remains dry.

- Place a tray beneath the wire rack on which the tikkas or any tandoori food is placed. Cover tray with aluminium foil, to collect the drippings of the tikkas etc.

- Always grease/brush the wire rack or grill nicely with oil to avoid the kebabs from sticking to the grill. If not properly greased, when you pick up the done food, the marinade comes off as it sticks to the grill .

- Cut the pieces of food according to the space in between the wires of the grill. If the distance between the wires of the rack is too wide, and there is a chance of your piece slipping, then cover the wire rack with a well greased aluminium foil.

- The size of the tikkas should not be too small, because after getting cooked they shrink. A very small piece after getting cooked can turn hard after some time.

- While skewering or placing pieces of chicken, mutton, fish or even vegetable, the pieces should be arranged such that there is atleast 1" gap between them so that each piece can get it's own space and heat all around to get cooked properly.

- While threading meat, the skewers should be pushed gently. They should be woven through the tikka. This way there are less chances of meat slipping down.

- When skewering delicate meats like fish and prawns or vegetables, it is advisable to use thinner skewers, then there is less chance of the vegetable or fish to break.

- Pastes like raw papaya paste, ginger-garlic paste, onion paste, coriander paste or chilli paste should be made with as little water as possible.

- To keep the tandoori food soft and succulent, baste food with some melted butter/ oil or sometimes with the left over marinade. To baste, just pour the oil/melted butter on the food that is being barbecued when it is a little more than half done.

- While grilling tikkas, turn them only after they are half done, otherwise they tend to break if they are shifted again & again. To check if meat is fully cooked, break a little. If it breaks off easily, it is done, otherwise it needs to be cooked more.

- If the mutton is not of very good quality, you may first pressure cook the mutton and then marinate the cooked mutton. Barbecue it at the time of Serving.

CHICKEN

- All boneless tikka recipes could be made with chicken with bones. Increase ¼ quantity of the marinade and all the other ingredients, if using chicken with bones and grill for a little longer, for about 20 minutes atleast.
- Cut the pieces of food according to the space in between the wires of the grill. If the distance between the wires of the rack is too wide, and there is a chance of your piece slipping, then cover the wire rack with a well greased aluminium foil.

- The size of the tikkas should not be too small, because after getting cooked they shrink. A very small piece after getting cooked can turn hard after some time.
- While skewering or placing pieces of chicken, mutton, fish or even vegetable, the pieces should be arranged such that there is atleast 1" gap between them so that each piece can get it's own space and heat all around to get cooked properly.
- Always place the tikkas or the kebabs on the grill or on the wire rack and never directly on a tray. When you place them on a tray, the liquid that drips while grilling keeps collecting around the food and keeps the food wet all the time. This prevents the tandoori food from getting crisp on the outside. Whereas, if the food is placed on the wire rack, the liquid drips down and food remains dry.

Til Tikka

Exotic, flavourful tikka coated with sesame seeds mixed with a green coriander paste.

Serves 4-5   *Picture on cover*

500 gms boneless chicken - cut into 1" pieces
¼ cup til (sesame seeds)

1ST MARINADE (MIX TOGETHER)
1 cup yogurt - hang in a muslin cloth for 1 hour
1 tbsp lemon juice or vinegar
seeds of 2 moti illaichi (black cardamom) - crushed
seeds of 4 chhoti illaichi (green cardamom)- crushed
¼ tsp jaiphal (nutmeg) powder
¼ tsp javetri (mace) powder
½ tsp freshly ground saboot kali mirch (black peppercorns)
2 tbsp oil
1 tsp salt, ¼ tsp chilli powder

GRIND TO A PASTE
3 green chillies, ½ cup fresh green coriander, a pinch of salt

BATTER
1 egg
¼ cup maida (plain flour)
1 tsp salt, a pinch of tandoori colour, optional

BASTING (POURING ON THE TIKKAS)
3 tbsp melted butter or oil, mixed with 2 tbsp til

1. Wash the chicken pieces and pat dry on a kitchen towel.
2. Marinate the chicken in the 1st marinade for ½ hour.
3. Grind green coriander and green chillies to a fine paste in a grinder.
4. Mix til and green paste and spread it in the plate. Keep mixture aside.
5. For the batter, beat egg, flour and salt in a bowl. Add colour if you wish.
6. Taking one tikka at a time, dip it in the prepared batter, coat it well.
7. Then roll the coated tikka in the til and green paste mixture. Keep aside.
8. Heat an electric oven at 180°C or a gas tandoor on gas at moderate flame. Grease the wire or grill rack generously with oil. Place the well coated chicken pieces on the greased grill or skewer the chicken pieces.
9. Roast for 10-15 minutes. Baste (pour) with oil mixed with til after 10 minutes or when the coating turns a little dry. Cook again for 5 minutes.
10. Serve with chilli garlic chutney (see page 119).

Mewa Seekh

Delicious rich seekh kebabs for special occasions. People consume them much more than expected, especially at a party.

Picture on page 1   *Serves 4 - 5*

½ kg (500 gm) keema (chicken mince)
1 cup dry bread crumbs
1 tsp oil
1 tbsp cornflour
½ tsp garam masala, ½ tsp salt, 1 egg white
2 tsp magaz (melon seeds) & 1 tbsp chironji (sunflower seeds) - dry roast on a tawa

GRIND TOGETHER
1" piece ginger, 6-8 flakes garlic, 2 green chillies, ¼ cup green coriander
10 kaju (cashewnuts)
8 badam (almonds) - blanched and peeled
5 kishmish (raisins), ½ tsp whole pista (pistachio)
¼ tsp jaiphal (nutmeg), ¼ tsp javetri (mace)
½ tbsp kachri powder

BASTING (POURING ON THE SEEKHS)
2 tbsp melted butter or oil

1. Wash the mince in a strainer and squeeze out all the excess water by pressing well. Grind the mince twice till smooth.
2. Roast magaz and chironji on a hot tawa. Cool.
3. Grind ginger, garlic, green chillies, coriander, kaju, badam, kishmish, pista, jaiphal, javetri, kachri and roasted chironji and magaz in a grinder. Remove from grinder to a big bowl.
4. Add bread crumbs, oil, cornflour, garam masala, salt and chicken mince. Mix well and marinate covered in the refrigerator for 4-5 hours or till serving time.
5. At serving time, heat an electric oven at 180°C or gas tandoor on moderate heat.
6. Grease a skewer and warm it a little on fire. Take a big ball of the mince mixture and hold the skewer carefully in the other hand. Press the mince on to the skewer very carefully. The mince will immediately stick to the slightly hot skewer. If the skewers are very cold the mince will not stick. Make one big seekh on the skewer. Repeat with the left over mince on all the other skewers.
7. Place the skewers in the hot oven or gas tandoor. Cook for 10-15 minutes or till done, rotating the skewers. When the seekhs get cooked, gently remove the kebab from the skewers with the help of a cloth. Cut each into 1" pieces to serve.

Malai Tikka

Kebabs that melt in your mouth. The number of people served by this recipe depends on the appetite of your guests. Men/Boys will consume much more particularly if they are served with drinks at a cocktail party.

Serves 6-7   *Picture on back cover*

500 gms boneless chicken - cut into 1½" pieces
OR
500 gms of chicken breasts (3) - cut into 2" pieces

MARINADE
¾ cup thick cream
¼ tsp green cardamom powder (seeds of 2-3 chhoti illaichi - crushed)
1 tsp white or black pepper powder
1 tsp garlic paste, 2 tsp ginger paste
3 tbsp cornflour
1 tbsp melted butter
½ tsp garam masala powder, ¼ tsp amchoor, ½ tsp jeera powder, 1½ tsp salt
2 green chillies - crushed, optional

BASTING (POURING ON THE KEBABS)
2 tbsp melted butter or oil

1. Mix all the ingredients of the marinade- cream, chhoti illaichi powder, white pepper, ginger-garlic paste, cornflour, melted butter, garam masala, amchoor, jeera powder, salt and green chillies.
2. Marinate chicken covered with a plastic wrap/cling film for 1 hour in the refrigerator.
3. Heat an oven at 180°C or heat a gas tandoor on gas for 15 minutes on low heat.
4. Place the well coated chicken pieces on the grill or skewer the chicken pieces. Roast for 10 minutes or until cooked, thoroughly basting (pouring) with melted butter or oil at least once in between. Roast for another 5 minutes.
5. Sprinkle chaat masala and serve hot with poodina chutney and arbi ka salad (see page 120) or garnished papad (see page 126).

Note:

- Grilling or roasting should be done on constant moderate heat, otherwise it toughens the protein of the meat, making the kebabs shrink and turn hard. Always grease the wire rack or grill nicely with oil to avoid the kebabs sticking to the grill.
- Cover the tray beneath the wire rack or the skewers with aluminium foil to collect the drippings of the tikkas.

Akbari Kebabs

Chicken breasts stuffed with a spiced cheese filling.

Picture on page 2   *Serves 4*

2 chicken breasts (300gm)

IST MARINADE
1 tbsp lemon juice, ½ tsp salt, ½ tsp red chilli powder

2ND MARINADE
1 cup thick curd - hung for 15-20 minutes
¼ cup thick cream
2 tbsp grated cheese
1 tsp shah jeera (black cumin) - roughly crushed
1 tbsp cornflour
1 tsp red chilli powder, 1 tsp salt, a pinch of haldi, 1 tsp garam masala
1 tbsp ginger-garlic paste
1 tbsp barbecue masala or tandoori masala (optional)
2 tbsp coriander - chopped

FILLING
1 onion - cut into rings & then cut rings into half, 1 tbsp coriander - chopped
1 tsp shah jeera (black cumin)
100 gm cheese - finely grated
1½ tbsp oil
1 tsp ginger-garlic paste, 1 tbsp coriander

1. Open the breast slices to get thin big pieces (you can ask your butcher to do it for you). Cut each breast into 4 long strips, about 1½" wide, to make rolls.
2. Wash and pat dry the chicken strips.
3. Marinate the chicken with the first marinade – salt, lemon juice and chilli powder.
4. Mix the ingredients of the 2nd marinade together in a bowl.
5. Pick up the chicken pieces from the lemon juice marinade and squeeze gently. Put them in the curd- cream marinade in the bowl.
6. For the filling, heat oil. Add shah jeera. Let it change colour. Add onion. Cook till onion turns soft. Add ginger-garlic paste and coriander. Cook for 1 minute. Remove from fire. Add cheese.
7. To make the kebab, take a strip of chicken. Place 1 tbsp of filling on one end of the chicken strip and roll it forward tightly to form a roll. Place the roll on the greased wire rack. Pat the remaining marinade on the rolls.
8. Heat an oven to 180°C. Grill for ½ hour, turning and basting with melted butter or oil after 15-20 minutes. Cook till tender.

Besani Murg Tangri

Delicious, pan fried chicken legs/tikkas coated with gram flour and curd.

Serves 3-4

400 gms chicken - cut into 1½" pieces or 6 legs (drumsticks)
¾ cup milk
1 tsp red chilli powder, ¾ tsp salt

GRIND TOGETHER TO A PASTE
½" piece ginger
2-3 flakes garlic
2 saboot kali mirch (peppercorns)
2 laung (cloves)
2 chhoti illaichi (green cardamoms)
1 tsp jeera (cumin seeds)
2 tsp saboot dhania (coriander seeds)
¾" stick dalchini
¾ tsp saunf (fennel)

COATING
8 tbsp besan
6 tbsp curd
1 tbsp chopped fresh dhania
½ tsp salt, ¼ tsp red chilli powder
¼ tsp ajwain (carom seeds)

1. Grind together ginger, garlic along with all the saboot masalas to a paste. Use a little water if required. Keep the ground paste aside.
2. Mix together ¾ cup milk with ¼ cup water. Heat and bring to a boil.
3. Add the above ground masala, 1 tsp red chilli powder and ¾ tsp salt.
4. Add chicken also to the milk. Give 1-2 boils. Cover and lower heat. Cook for 8-10 minutes or till the chicken is tender. Increase the heat and cook till completely dry. Remove from fire. Cool.
5. To the cooked chicken add all the coating ingredients. Mix well.
6. Heat 3 tbsp oil in a pan and fry 2-3 pieces at a time to a golden brown colour.
7. Sprinkle some freshly ground pepper and serve hot with chilli garlic chutney (see page 119) and khatti arbi ka salad (see page 120).

Methi Tikka

Fenugreek blends wonderfully with chicken.

Serves 4 -5

½ kg boneless chicken - cut into 1" pieces

1ST MARINADE
juice of 1 lemon
½ tsp salt
½ tsp pepper
3 tsp ginger-garlic paste
2 tbsp oil

2ND MARINADE
1 cup thick curd - hang for 30 minutes in a muslin cloth
2 tsp dhania powder
3 tbsp kasoori methi (dry fenugreek leaves)
2 tbsp cornflour, 1 tsp besan
¼ tsp chilli powder, 1 tsp salt
1 tsp oil

BASTING (POURING ON THE TIKKAS)
1 tbsp oil
½ tsp methi daana (fenugreek seeds), 1 tbsp kasoori methi

1. Wash the chicken pieces and pat dry on a kitchen towel.
2. Marinate the chicken pieces in the 1st marinade- lemon juice, salt, pepper, ginger-garlic and oil for ½ hour.
3. In a bowl mix the ingredients of 2nd marinade- curd, dhania powder, kasoori methi, cornflour, besan, chilli powder, salt and oil. Pick up the chicken pieces from the lemon juice marinade and squeeze gently. Mix it with the curd marinade in the bowl. Leave it to marinate for 1 hour in the refrigerator. Cover with a plastic wrap/cling film.
4. For basting, heat oil, add fenugreek seeds, let them turn brown. Sieve it through a steel sieve or strainer. Add kasoori methi to oil.
5. Heat an oven at 180°C or heat a gas tandoor on gas for 15 minutes on low heat. Place the well coated chicken pieces on the greased grill or skewer the chicken pieces.
6. Roast for 15 minutes. Baste (pour) with oil after 10 minutes or when the coating turns a little dry. Cook again for 5 minutes.
7. Serve with chilli garlic chutney (see page 119) and peanut cabbage relish (see page 121).

Shaan-E-Murg

Strips of chicken breast rolled in a black cumin flavoured paneer stuffing.

Serves 5-6

2 chicken breasts (300 gm)

MARINADE
1 tbsp lemon juice, ¼ tsp salt, ½ tsp red chilli powder, 2 tbsp oil

COATING BATTER
1 egg, 1 tbsp maida (flour), 3 tbsp cornflour, a pinch of salt

FILLING
75 gm paneer - grated
1 fresh pineapple slice - finely chopped
1 tsp shah jeera (black cumin)
1 small onion - finely chopped
2 tsp kaju (cashewnuts) - roughly chopped
2 green chillies - deseeded and chopped, 2 tbsp chopped coriander
¼ tsp bhuna jeera (roasted cumin), ¼ tsp chilli powder, ½ tsp salt or to taste
1½ tsp melted butter or oil

BASTING (POURING ON THE KEBABS)
2 tbsp melted butter or oil

1. Open the breast slices to get thin big pieces (you can ask your butcher to do it for you). Cut each breast into long strips, about 1½" wide, to make rolls (approx. 3 or 4 strips depending on the size of the breasts).
2. Wash and pat dry the chicken strips.
3. Marinate the chicken with the marinade - lemon juice, salt, oil and chilli powder for 1 hour in the refrigerator. Cover with a plastic wrap/cling film.
4. For the filling, heat butter. Add shah jeera. Let it change colour. Add onion. Cook till onion turns soft.
5. Add kaju, green chillies, coriander, bhuna jeera, chilli powder, salt and paneer. Cook for 1 minute. Remove from fire. Add pineapple pieces.
6. For the batter, beat egg. Add cornflour, flour & salt to make a batter. Whisk well.
7. To make the kebab rolls take a strip of chicken. Place 1 tbsp of filling on one end of the strip and roll it forward tightly to form a roll. Dip this roll gently in the prepared egg batter & place it on greased grill. Repeat with the rest of the strips.
8. Heat an oven at 180°C or heat a gas tandoor for 15 minutes on low heat. Place the roll on the greased wire rack or grill. Grill for ½ hour on a greased wire rack turning and basting with butter or oil after 20 minutes. Cook till tender. Serve.

Tangri Kebabs

Chicken legs marinated in a cream-curd mixture.

Picture on facing page   *Serves 4*

8 drumsticks (chicken legs)

1ST MARINADE
2-3 tbsp lemon juice, ½ tsp salt, or to taste, ½ tsp red chilli powder

2ND MARINADE
1 cup thick curd - hang for 15 minutes
¼ cup thick cream
1 egg
1 tbsp cornflour
2 tbsp ginger-garlic paste
1 tbsp chopped coriander
¾ tsp salt

BASTING (POURING ON THE KEBABS)
2 tbsp melted butter or oil

1. Wash and pat dry the chicken pieces. Make 2 incisions (not too deep cuts) on each drumstick.
2. Marinate the pieces with the first marinade – salt, red chilli and lemon juice for ½ hour.
3. Mix cream, egg, cornflour, ginger-garlic paste, salt and coriander to the curd.
4. Pick up the chicken pieces discarding the lemon juice. Marinate the chicken pieces in the curd mixture for 2-3 hours or even more, but refrigerate while being marinated. You may marinate the chicken overnight too.
5. Heat an oven at 180°C or heat a gas tandoor on moderate heat for 15 minutes.
6. Grill the marinated chicken pieces on a greased wire grill, turning once in between and basting the chicken legs with oil or butter. Grill till tender for about 15 minutes. You can check if the chicken is soft with a knife also.
7. Serve hot sprinkled with some chaat masala and lemon juice.
8. Serve with mint chutney and mixed green relish (see page 119) or garnished papad (seepage 126). Garnish with onion rings.

Note: Grilling or roasting should be done on constant moderate heat, and not on very high heat. High heat toughens the proteins of the meat or paneer, making the kebabs shrink and turn hard.

Dhania Fish Tikka : Recipe on page 72, Tangri Kebabs ➤

Moong Phali Kebabs

A combination of peanut and tamarind makes a delicious kebab.

Serves 4-6

500 gm boneless chicken - cut into 2" pieces

1ST MARINADE
2 tbsp lemon juice or vinegar
½ tsp salt, ½ tsp chilli powder
1 tbsp oil

2ND MARINADE
1 cup thick curd - hang for ½ hour
6 tbsp peanuts (moongphali) and 2 tbsp milk
a lemon sized ball of imli (tamarind) (2 tbsp pulp)
2 tbsp ginger- garlic paste
1½ tsp salt, ½ tsp chilli powder

TADKA(TEMPRING)
2 tbsp oil
1 tsp rai (mustard seeds), 1 tsp jeera
4-5 dry red chillies - broken into bits
15- 20 curry patta- chopped

1. Wash the chicken pieces and pat dry on a kitchen towel.
2. Marinate the pieces in the 1st marinade- lemon juice, salt, chilli powder and oil for ½ hour.
3. For tamarind pulp, boil ¼ cup water with a lemon sized ball tamarind. Strain and keep aside.
4. Grind peanuts with 2 tbsp milk in a blender to form a paste. Keep aside.
5. For tadka, heat 2 tbsp oil in a pan. Add rai, jeera, dry red chillies and curry patta. Let jeera turn golden. Remove from fire. Keep tadka mixture aside.
6. Mix hung curd with ginger- garlic paste, peanut paste, tamarind pulp, salt, chilli powder and the tadka.
7. Heat an oven at 180°C or heat a gas tandoor for 15 minutes on low heat.
8. Place the well coated chicken pieces on the greased grill or skewer the chicken pieces. Roast for 15 minutes or until cooked.
9. Serve hot with poodina chutney (see page 119) & arbi ka salad (see page 120) or garnished papad (see page 126). Sprinkle chaat masala.

Note: There is no need for basting as the marinades are wet themselves. But still if the kebabs turn dry during cooking then baste with 1 tbsp oil.

Banjaara Tandoori Tangri

Makes 8   *Picture on page 86*

8 drumsticks (chicken legs)

1ST MARINADE
2-3 tbsp lemon juice
1 tsp salt or to taste, 1 tsp red chilli powder

2ND MARINADE
1 cup thick curd - hang for ½ hour in a muslin cloth
¼ cup thick cream
1 egg
1 tbsp cornflour
2 tbsp ginger-garlic paste
¾ tsp salt
¼ tsp kala namak (black salt)
1 tsp shah jeera (black cumin) - crushed
¼ tsp jaiphal (nutmeg) powder
1 tbsp kasoori methi, 2 tbsp chopped coriander
a pinch of orange colour

1. Wash and pat dry the chicken pieces. Make 2 incisions (not too deep cuts) on each drumstick.
2. Marinate the pieces with the 1st marinade – salt, red chilli powder and lemon juice for ½ hour.
3. Add all ingredients of the 2nd marinade- curd, cream, egg, cornflour, ginger-garlic paste, salt, kala namak, shah jeera, jaiphal powder, kasoori methi and coriander. Add enough colour to get a light orange colour.
4. Pick up the chicken pieces discarding the lemon juice. Marinate the chicken pieces in the curd mixture for 2-3 hours or even more, but refrigerate while being marinated. You may marinate the chicken overnight too.
5. Heat an oven at 180°C or heat a gas tandoor for 15 minutes on low heat.
6. Grill the marinated chicken pieces on a greased wire grill, turning once in between and basting the chicken legs with oil or butter. Grill till tender for about 15 minutes.
7. Serve hot sprinkled with some chaat masala and lemon juice.
8. Serve with dahi poodina chutney (see page 118) and mixed green relish (see page 121). Garnish with onion rings.

Kebab Kali Mirch

A quick kebab which can be served as the main dish or a snack.

Serves 4

1 chicken (800 gm) - cut into 12 pieces
6-7 tbsp butter (preferably Amul)
2 tsp grated cheese (mozzarella)
3 tbsp grated ginger
1 tsp salt
2 tsp chopped coriander
2 tsp freshly ground pepper (saboot kali mirch) - crushed
2 tbsp thick cream

GARNISHING
some fresh coriander - chopped
3-4 peppercorns (saboot kali mirch) - crushed
3-4 tbsp lemon juice (adjust to taste)

BASTING (POURING ON THE KEBABS)
2 tbsp melted butter

1. Heat butter on medium flame. (If the heat is high, the butter will burn).
2. Add grated ginger. Fry on medium heat till slightly brown.
3. Add coriander, chicken, salt and pepper. Fry till chicken changes colour, for about 3-4 minutes.
4. Remove from fire. Cool. Add thick cream and cheese. Mix well.
5. Heat an electric oven at 180°C or a gas tandoor on gas for 15 minutes at moderate flame.
6. Place the well coated chicken pieces on the grill or skewer the chicken pieces. Roast for 10 minutes.
7. Baste (pour) with oil after 8-10 minutes or when the coating turns a little dry. Roast for another 5- 10 minutes. Check whether the chicken is cooked by inserting a knife when the chicken is in the oven. If the knife goes in softly without any pressure, then the chicken is cooked.
8. To serve, add lemon juice and sprinkle coarsely pounded pepper and fresh coriander.
9. Serve with chilli garlic chutney (see page 119) and garnished papad (see page 126).

Note: Grilling or roasting should be done on constant moderate heat, and not on very high heat. High heat toughens the proteins of the chicken, making the kebabs shrink and turn hard.

Chicken Seekh Kebab

Serves 6-8

500 gm chicken mince (keema)
2 onions - sliced
8-10 garlic flakes
1" piece ginger
1 tbsp khus khus (poppy seeds) - soaked for 15 minutes in water
1½ tbsp broken cashewnuts
1 tbsp chopped green coriander
1 tsp garam masala
½ tsp red chilli powder
1 tsp salt to taste
2 tbsp oil

FOR GARNISHING
lemon, chat masala, onion rings

BASTING (POURING ON THE SEEKHS)
2 tbsp oil

1. Place the mince in a strainer. Wash in the strainer. Press out the excess water.
2. Heat oil in a kadhai and deep fry the onions till golden brown. Drain with a slotted spoon and cool.
3. Grind the browned onions, ginger, garlic, cashewnuts and drained khus khus to a smooth thick paste.
4. Put the mince, onion paste, garam masala, chilli powder and salt in a mixer blender. Grind well to get a sticky consistency. Remove the mixture to a bowl.
5. Add chopped coriander. Refrigerate for atleast 2-3 hours for the flavours to penetrate the mince.
6. Heat an oven at 180°C or heat a gas tandoor on gas for 15 minutes on low heat.
7. Take a big ball of the mince mixture and hold a well greased hot skewer carefully in the other hand. Press the mince on to a skewer. The mince will immediately stick to the skewer. If the skewers are cold the mince will not stick. Make one big seekh on the skewer. Repeat with the left over mince on all the other skewers.
8. Place the skewers in the hot oven or gas tandoor. Cook for 10-15 minutes or till done, rotating the skewers. When the seekhs get cooked, gently remove the kebab from the skewers with the help of a cloth. Cut each into 1" pieces to serve.
9. Sprinkle lemon juice and chat masala on the kebabs and onions and serve with onion rings and khatti meethi chutney and sirke waale pyaaz (see page 120).

Chicken Tikka

Picture on page 117   *Serves 4*

2-3 breasts of chicken or 500 gm boneless chicken - cut into 2" pieces (8-12 pieces)

1ST MARINADE
2 tbsp vinegar or lemon juice
¼ tsp salt
½ tsp chilli powder

2ND MARINADE
6 tbsp thick hung curd (hang about ¾ cup curd)
3 tbsp thick malai or cream
2 tsp ginger-garlic paste
½ tsp tandoori masala (optional)
¼ tsp black salt (kala namak)
½ tsp garam masala powder
¼ tsp red chilli powder
¾-1 tsp salt, or to taste
2-3 drops of red colour
2 tsp oil
some chaat masala and lemon juice to sprinkle

BASTING (POURING ON THE TIKKAS)
2 tbsp melted butter

1. Wash the chicken pieces and pat dry on a kitchen towel.
2. Marinate the pieces in the 1st marinade for ½ hour.
3. In a bowl mix all ingredients of 2nd marinade- curd, cream, ginger-garlic paste, tandoori masala, black salt, garam masala, red chill powder, colour, salt and oil.
4. Remove the chicken pieces from the 1st marinade. Pat dry slightly. Add to the curd mixture and marinate for 6-8 hours in the refrigerator.
5. Heat an electric oven at 180°C or a gas tandoor on gas at moderate flame. Place the well coated chicken pieces on the greased grill or skewer the chicken pieces.
6. Roast for 15 minutes. Baste (pour) with melted butter after 10 minutes or when the coating turns a little dry. Grill again for 5 minutes.
7. Sprinkle some chaat masala and lemon juice.
8. Serve hot with sirke waale pyaaz (see page 120) and peanut-cabbage relish (see page 121).

Note: The size of the tikkas should not be too small, because after getting cooked they shrink. A very small piece after getting cooked can turn hard after some time.

Badaami Tangri

Serves 4

8 drumsticks (chicken legs)

1ST MARINADE
2-3 tbsp lemon juice
½ tsp salt, or to taste, ½ tsp red chilli powder

2ND MARINADE
¾ cup thick curd - hang for 15 minutes
½ cup thick cream
2 tbsp almonds - blanched (soaked in hot water and peeled) and ground to a paste
2 tsp kasoori methi (dry fenugreek leaves)
1 tbsp cornflour
2 tbsp ginger-garlic paste
¾ tsp salt
2 tbsp chopped coriander

BASTING (POURING ON THE TANGRI)
3 tbsp melted butter mixed with 1 tsp white pepper and 2 tsp kasoori methi

1. Wash and pat dry the chicken pieces. Make 2 incisions (not too deep cuts) on each drumstick.
2. Marinate the pieces with the first marinade – salt, red chilli and lemon juice for ½ hour.
3. Mix curd, cream, almond paste, kasoori methi, cornflour, ginger-garlic paste, salt and coriander in a bowl.
4. Pick up the chicken pieces discarding the lemon juice. Marinate the chicken pieces in the curd mixture for 2-3 hours or even more, but refrigerate while being marinated. You may marinate the chicken overnight too.
5. Heat an electric oven at 180°C or a gas tandoor on gas at moderate flame for 10 minutes. Grill the marinated chicken pieces on a greased wire grill.
6. Melt some butter and mix some white pepper and kasoori methi in it. Turn the chicken once in between and baste (pour) with this melted butter to flavour the chicken. Grill till tender for about 15-20 minutes.
7. Serve hot sprinkled with some chaat masala and lemon juice.
8. Serve with dahi poodina chutney (see page 118). Garnish with onion rings.

Note: While skewering or placing pieces of any meat or even vegetable, arrange leaving atleast 1" gap between them so that each piece get it's own space and heat to get cooked.

Saunfiya Kebabs

Gives 6-8 pieces

200 gms boneless (skinless) chicken - cut in 1½"- 2 " pieces
1 tsp garlic paste
1 tbsp chopped coriander
¾ tsp saunf (fennel) - crushed
¾ tsp salt
1 tsp amchoor (dry mango) powder
1 tsp degi mirch
¼ tsp jaiphal (nutmeg) powder
3 tbsp cream or malai
1 tbsp cornflour

BASTING (POURING ON THE KEBABS)
1 tbsp melted butter

GARNISH
1 tsp chaat masala

1. Place chicken pieces in a bowl. Add garlic paste, coriander, saunf, salt, amchoor, degi mirch, jaiphal, cream and cornflour. Mix well. Let it marinate for 1-2 hours at room temperature.
2. Heat an electric oven at 180°C or a gas tandoor on gas at moderate flame. Place the well coated chicken pieces on the greased grill or skewer the chicken pieces.
3. Roast for 15 minutes. Baste (pour) with oil after 10 minutes or when the coating turns a little dry. Cook again for 5 minutes.
4. Sprinkle some chaat masala and serve with and til chutney and khatti arbi ka salad (see page 120) or garnished papad (see page 126).

Note:
- Always grease/brush the wire rack or grill nicely with oil to avoid the kebabs from sticking to the grill.
- Cut the pieces of food according to the space in between the wires of the grill. If the distance between the wires of the rack is too wide, and there is a chance of your piece slipping, then cover the wire rack with a well greased aluminium foil.
- The size of the tikkas should not be too small, because after getting cooked they shrink. A very small piece after getting cooked can turn hard after some time.
- While skewering or placing pieces of chicken, mutton, fish or even vegetable, the pieces should be arranged such that there is atleast 1" gap between them so that each piece can get it's own space and heat all around to get cooked properly.

Pista Murg Tikka

Cubes of chicken marinated with pistachio paste and hung curd.

Serves 6

½ kg (500 gm) boneless chicken - cut into 2" pieces

MARINADE
**4 tbsp pista - soaked in warm water, peeled and ground to a green paste
with 2 tbsp water**
½ cup dahi (yogurt) - hang for 15-20 minutes in a muslin cloth
3 tbsp thick cream
2 tbsp ginger - garlic paste
½ tsp garam masala
½ tsp shah jeera (black cumin)
1 tsp red chilli powder, 1 tsp salt
3 tbsp cornflour
3 tbsp oil

BASTING (POURING ON THE TIKKAS)
3 tbsp oil

GARNISH
a pinch of kesar (saffron) - soaked in 1 tbsp milk
1 tsp pistas - chopped

1. Mix all the ingredients of the marinade and put the tikkas in it. Leave aside for 4-5 hours in the refrigerator.
2. Oil a wire rack of the oven. Place the tikkas on it, leaving behind the extra marinade.
3. Place the tikkas in the oven at 180°C and cook for 10 minutes. Baste the tikkas with some oil and grill for another 5-10 minutes. Transfer to a serving platter.
4. Serve with poodina chutney (see page 119) and onion rings seasoned with salt and red chilli powder.
5. On a slow fire heat the leftover marinade. When it begins to thicken, add the saffron soaked in milk and cook for 1-2 minutes. Pour over the tikkas. Sprinkle with chopped pistas and serve with poodina chutney (see page 119).

Note: Always place the tikkas or the kebabs on the grill or on the wire rack and never directly on a tray. When you place them on a tray, the liquid that drips while grilling keeps collecting around the food and keeps the food wet all the time. This prevents the tandoori food from getting crisp on the outside. Whereas, if the food is placed on the wire rack, the liquid drips down & food remains dry.

Peshawari Murg Kebab

Tikka prepared using rich ingredients and spices.

Serves 4-5

300 gms boneless chicken or 2 chicken breasts - cut into 2" pieces (8-12 pieces)
some chat masala, lemon juice and coriander leaves

1ST MARINADE
2 tbsp vinegar or lemon juice
¼ tsp salt
½ tsp red chilli powder

2ND MARINADE
½ cup thick curd - hang for ½ hour in a muslin cloth
3 tbsp thick malai or cream
2 tbsp badam (almond) paste (soak, peel and grind almonds)
1 tbsp cornflour
2 tsp ginger-garlic paste
1 tsp shah jeera (black cumin) - roughly crushed
¼ tsp kala namak (black salt)
½ tsp garam masala powder
a pinch of tandoori red colour
¼ tsp red chilli powder
1 tsp salt or to taste

BASTING (POURING ON THE KEBABS)
2 tbsp oil

1. Wash the chicken pieces and pat dry on a kitchen towel.
2. Marinate the pieces in the 1st marinade - lime juice, salt, chilli powder for ½ hour.
3. In a bowl mix curd, cream, badam paste, kala namak, ginger-garlic paste, garam masala, red chilli powder, colour and salt to taste. Keep curd mixture aside.
4. Remove the chicken pieces from the 1st marinade. Pat dry slightly. Add to the curd mixture and marinate for 6-8 hours in the fridge.
5. Heat an electric oven at 180°C or a gas tandoor on gas at moderate flame. Rub oil generously on the wire rack or grill of the tandoor or oven. Place the chicken pieces on the wire rack and grill for 15 minutes or till pieces are light brown. Baste (pour) with oil turning sides and grill for another 5-10 minutes or till tender. Sprinkle chat masala and lemon juice.
6. Serve hot with poodina chutney (see page 119), garnished with coriander leaves.

Kesari Tikka

Saffron! The aristocrat of spices - fragrant and burnished gold in colour, straight from the Kashmir valley.

Serves 4-6

½ kg boneless chicken - cut into tikka pieces (2" pieces)

1 ST MARINADE
1 tbsp lemon juice, ½ tsp salt, ½ tsp red chilli powder

2ND MARINADE
1 cup yogurt - hang in a muslin cloth for ½ hour
¼ tsp kesar (saffron)
2 tsp milk
8 chhoti illaichi (green cardamoms) - crushed
1 tsp salt
3 tbsp oil

BASTING
3 tbsp melted butter

1. Soak kesar in 2 tsp of milk for ½ hour.
2. Wash the chicken pieces and pat dry on a kitchen towel.
3. Marinate the chicken with the first marinade – salt, lemon juice and chilli powder for ½ hour.
4. Mix the ingredients of the 2nd marinade together in a bowl- curd, soaked kesar, chhoti illaichi, salt and oil.
5. Pick up the chicken pieces from the lemon juice marinade and squeeze gently. Put them in the curd-kesar marinade in the bowl. Marinate for 6-8 hours in the refrigerator.
6. Heat an electric oven at 180°C or a gas tandoor on gas at moderate flame.
7. Place the well coated chicken pieces on the greased grill or skewer the chicken pieces.
8. Roast for 20 minutes, thoroughly basting with oil after 10 minutes or when the coating turns a little dry. Cook again for 5-10 minutes.
9. Serve hot with sirke waale pyaaz (see page 120) and peanut-cabbage relish (see page 121).

Note: The size of the tikkas should not be too small, because after getting cooked they shrink. A very small piece after getting cooked can turn hard after some time.

Chicken Tikka Masala

Dry chicken tikka covered with thick masala. It can be served as a snack or as a side dish with the main meal.

Serves 4

½ kg cooked chicken tikka
(prepare chicken tikka as given on page 24)

MASALA
2 tomatoes - blanched (put in hot water and peeled) and chopped
1 onion - sliced
½ cup coconut milk
¼ tsp sarson (mustard seeds)
¼ tsp kalonji (black onion seeds)
2 green chillies - finely chopped
2 tbsp mint leaves - finely chopped
2 tbsp coriander - finely chopped
1½ tbsp lemon juice
½ tsp garam masala
½ tsp salt
3 tbsp oil

1. Prepare chicken tikka as given on page 24.
2. For the masala – heat 1½ tbsp oil, add sarson and kalonji. Wait for 30 seconds. Add onions and saute over medium heat until golden brown.
3. Add crushed garlic and chopped green chillies. Mix well.
4. Add tomatoes, cook till oil separates.
5. Add coconut milk and bring to a boil, stirring continuously. Lower heat and cook for 5-10 minutes, or until thick. Keep masala aside.
6. At the time of serving, remove the cooked chicken tikka from the skewers and add to the masala.
7. Add chopped mint, coriander, lemon juice, salt and garam masala.
8. Serve with dahi poodina chutney (see page 118) and mixed green relish.

Note: To prepare fish tikka masala, make fish tikka as given on page 75 and prepare the same masala and mix the fish tikka with it.

Dakshin Kebabs

A combination of chicken with South Indian ingredients - curry leaves and coconut.

Serves 4-5

500 gms boneless chicken - cut into 2" pieces (8-12 pieces)

1ST MARINADE
2 tbsp lemon juice or vinegar
2 tbsp ginger-garlic paste
20- 25 curry leaves - finely chopped
3-4 green chillies - grind to a paste
½ tsp pepper
½ tsp salt

2ND MARINADE
1 cup dahi (yogurt) - hang in a muslin cloth for ½ hour
¼ cup grated coconut
1½ tbsp saboot dhania (coriander seeds)
½ tsp salt, ½ tsp red chilli powder

TO SPRINKLE
½ tsp dhania powder

1. Wash and pat dry the chicken pieces.
2. Marinate the pieces with the first marinade — lemon juice, ginger-garlic paste, chopped curry leaves, green chilli paste, salt and pepper for ½ hour.
3. Grind coconut and saboot dhania in a spice grinder to a paste.
4. Mix yogurt, salt, red chilli powder, coconut-coriander paste. Add the marinated chicken pieces to the yogurt mixture.
5. Marinate the chicken pieces in this mixture for 2-3 hours.
6. Heat an electric oven at 180°C or a gas tandoor on gas at moderate flame. Oil the wire rack of the oven. Place the tikkas on it. Cook for 15 minutes or till tender. Brush some oil after 10 minutes when the coating turns a little dry. Grill for another 5 minutes till tender.
7. Transfer to a serving platter, sprinkle dhania powder. Serve hot with instant khatti mithi chutney (see page 118) and onion rings.

Note: Do not keep the size of the pieces of the tikkas too small, because after getting cooked the size decreases. A very small piece after getting cooked can turn hard after some time.

Kastoori Kebab

An egg coated kebab, spiced with royal cumin and flavoured with cardamom.

Serves 8-10

500 gm boneless chicken mince (keema)
2 tbsp butter

1ST MARINADE
1½ tbsp ginger-garlic paste
1½ tbsp lemon juice or vinegar, ½ tsp salt

2ND MARINADE
6 tbsp besan, 5 tbsp bread crumbs
1 tsp white pepper powder
1 tsp ginger - finely chopped
1 tsp chhoti illaichi powder (green cardamom powder)
4 tbsp chopped coriander
½ tsp salt, ½ tsp red chilli powder, 1 tsp oil

BATTER
2 eggs
½ tsp shah jeera (black cumin seeds), ¼ tsp salt
½ tsp kesar (saffron)- soaked in 1 tbsp milk

BASTING
2 tbsp melted butter

1. Wash the mince in a strainer. Press well to squeeze out the water well.
2. Marinate mince with 1st marinade- salt, vinegar and ginger-garlic for ½ hour.
3. Heat 1 tbsp butter in a kadhai. Add besan and cook on low heat till golden brown. Remove from fire. Keep aside 3 tsp roasted besan separately.
4. To the rest of the besan add bread crumbs, white pepper powder, chopped ginger, chhoti illaichi powder, coriander, salt, chilli powder, oil and the marinated mince.
5. Shape the mince into flat tikkis.
6. For batter, mix the eggs with the reserved 3 tsp besan, jeera, salt and kesar. Whisk well.
7. Taking one tikki at a time, roll it in the egg mixture till well coated.
8. Heat 3 tbsp oil on a tawa or a shallow pan. Shallow fry on medium heat till light golden on both sides. Keep on low heat till the mince gets cooked properly and it turns brown (for about 8-10 minutes).
9. Sprinkle chaat masala and serve hot with poodina chutney and arbi ka salad (see page 120).

Cheesy Murg Tikka

These are not orange coloured like the tandoori tikkas. Cheese and eggs are added to the marinade to make the tikkas soft.

Serves 4

500 gm boneless chicken - cut into 2" pieces

1ST MARINADE
2 tbsp lemon juice or vinegar
2 tbsp ginger-garlic paste
½ tsp salt

2ND MARINADE
½ cup thick curd - hang for 15 minutes in a muslin cloth
¼ cup thick cream
2 cubes (40 gm) cheddar cheese (Britannia) - finely grated
1 egg, 1 tbsp cornflour
2 tbsp finely chopped green chillies
2 tbsp finely chopped coriander leaves

BASTING
4 tbsp melted butter or oil

1. Wash and pat dry the chicken pieces.
2. Marinate the tikkas with the first marinade — salt, lemon juice or vinegar and ginger-garlic paste for ½ hour.
3. Mix cream, cheese, egg, cornflour, green chillies and coriander to the curd.
4. Marinate the chicken pieces in this mixture for 1 hour.
5. Heat an oven at 180°C or heat a gas tandoor for 15 minutes on low heat. Place the well coated chicken pieces on the greased grill or skewer the chicken pieces.
6. Roast for 15 minutes. Baste (pour) with oil after 10 minutes or when the coating turns a little dry. Cook again for 5 minutes.
7. Serve hot with chutney or onion rings and garnished papad (see page 126).

Note:
- Grilling or roasting should be done on constant moderate heat, otherwise it toughens the protein of the meat, making the kebabs shrink and turn hard. Always grease the wire rack or grill nicely with oil to avoid the kebabs sticking to the grill.
- To check whether the chicken is cooked or not insert a knife when the chicken is in the oven. If the knife goes in softly without any pressure then chicken is cooked.
- While skewering or placing pieces of chicken, mutton, fish or even vegetable, the pieces should be such arranged that there is atleast 1" gap between them so that each piece can get it's own space and heat all around to get cooked.

Tandoori Chicken

An all time favourite of not only Punjabis but of all the people fond of good food.

Serves 4-5

1 small sized chicken (800 gm) - cut into 8 pieces
1 cup thick curd- hang in a muslin cloth for ½ hour
2 tbsp maida (plain flour), 2 tbsp oil
3 tsp ginger-garlic paste
a pinch of orange red colour
½ tsp jeera powder
½ tsp dhania powder
½ tsp garam masala powder, ½ tsp tandoori masala
1½ tsp amchoor powder
1½ tsp salt, 1 tsp red chilli powder
4 tbsp oil for basting (pouring on top)

1. Mix curd, maida, colour and all other ingredients. Add enough colour to get a bright orange colour.
2. Wash chicken. Squeeze out all excess water. Pat dry on a clean kitchen towel.
3. Marinate chicken in the curd mixture for 2-3 hours in the refrigerator.
4. Rub the wire rack of the oven with oil and place the marinated chicken on it, so that the extra marinade can drip down from the grill. If the chicken is placed in a dish or a tray, the extra marinade and liquid keep collecting around the chicken pieces and hence they do not turn dry and crisp.
5. Grill for 8-10 minutes in an oven at 180°C. Overturn again, baste (pour) with oil and grill for another 10-12 minutes or till tender and crisp.
6. Serve hot garnished with onion rings and garnished papad (see page 126).

Note:
- Instead of a full chicken only drumsticks (legs) can be made. They are called tangdi kebabs. After grilling, wrap a piece of aluminium foil at the end of each leg. Besides looking nice, it is also convenient for holding and eating the chicken leg.
- Boneless chicken cut into 1½"-2" pieces can be cooked in a similar manner to get chicken tikka.
- The grilled chicken can be added to an onion-tomato masala for a tikka masala dish.

Grilled Yogurt Tikka

The garlic-ginger-chilli paste added to the yogurt marinade makes it spicy and delicious.

Serves 4-6

400 gm boneless chicken- cut into 2" pieces
5 tbsp maida (plain flour), ½ tsp salt and ½ tsp pepper

IST MARINADE
1 tbsp lemon juice, ½ tsp salt, ½ tsp red chilli powder

GRIND TOGETHER TO A PASTE
8-10 flakes garlic, 3" piece ginger
2-3 red or green chillies

2ND MARINADE
1 cup thick curd - hung for 15-20 minutes
2 tbsp thick cream, 2 tbsp grated cheese
1 tsp shah jeera (black cumin) - roughly crushed
1 tsp red chilli powder, 1 tsp salt
a pinch of haldi, 1 tsp garam masala
1 tbsp ginger-garlic paste
1 tbsp barbecue masala or tandoori masala (optional)
2 tbsp green coriander - chopped
1 tsp garam masala
2 tbsp oil

BASTING
2 tbsp oil

1. Wash and pat dry the chicken tikkas.
2. Marinate the chicken with the first marinade –lemon juice, salt and chilli powder and the freshly ground garlic-ginger-chilli paste for ½ hour.
3. Mix the ingredients of the 2nd marinade together in a bowl.
4. Pick up the chicken pieces from the lemon juice marinade and squeeze gently. Put them in the prepared 2nd marinade of curd and cream in the bowl.
5. Mix the maida with ¼ tsp salt and ½ tsp pepper. Spread it evenly on a plate. Press or pat chicken pieces on the maida on both the sides.
6. Heat an electric oven at 180°C or a gas tandoor on gas at moderate flame. Rub oil generously on the wire rack or grill of the tandoor or oven. Place the chicken pieces on the wire rack and grill for 15 minutes or till pieces are light brown. Baste (pour) with oil turning sides and grill for another 5-10 minutes or till tender.
7. Garnish with mint leaves and serve hot with boiled vegetables.

Chinese Chicken Tikka

Tikka cooked with Chinese ingredients, an unusual combination.

Picture on facing page   Serves 4

2-3 breasts of chicken or 500 gm boneless chicken - cut into 2" pieces (8-12 pieces)
2 capsicums - cut into 1" pieces, 2 onions - cut into 8 pieces
1 tbsp lemon juice
½ tsp salt
2-3 dry, red chillies - crushed
½ tsp ajinomoto
3 tbsp vinegar, 2 tsp soya sauce
1½ tsp red chilli sauce, 2 tbsp tomato ketchup
1 tbsp white or red wine
1 egg white
4 tsp maida
4 tbsp cornflour
2 tsp ginger-garlic paste
1 tsp salt
1 tsp freshly ground pepper
3 tsp oil

BASTING (TO POUR ON THE TIKKAS)
2 tbsp oil

1. Wash the chicken pieces and pat dry on a kitchen towel.
2. Mix all the ingredients in a bowl- vinegar, soya sauce, chilli sauce, tomato ketchup, wine, egg white, ajinomoto, cornflour, ginger-garlic paste, salt, pepper, maida and oil. Mix well.
3. Add onion, capsicum and the tikka pieces. Mix well and marinate the chicken for 1 hour in the refrigerator.
4. Remove the capsicum pieces from the mixture and keep aside.
5. Heat an electric oven at 180°C or a gas tandoor on gas at moderate flame. Grease the grill or wire rack of the oven or tandoor and first place the well coated chicken and onions only on the grill. Grill for about 15 minutes, till the edges start to change colour.
6. After the chicken is almost done, put the capsicum also on the wire rack with the chicken etc. Baste (pour) with oil and grill for another 5 minutes.
7. Serve hot with chilli garlic chutney (see page 119) and peanut cabbage relish (see page 121).

Masala Chops : Recipe on page 48, Chilli garlic chutney : Recipe on page 119
Chinese Chicken Tikka ➤

MUTTON

- Mutton should be marinated for **atleast 4 hours** to get soft kebabs and tikkas.But if the mutton is marinated for too long with these, the meat tends to get mushy and the kebabs turn extra soft and break on cooking.

- A little tenderizer like **kachri powder** or **raw papaya paste** is important to get soft and delicious kebabs (Readymade kachri powder is easily available in shops).

- Always buy very good quality mutton for making tandoori food, otherwise you might have a tough time trying to cook it fully.

- While skewering or placing pieces of mutton, the pieces should be arranged such that there is atleast **1" gap** between them so that each piece can get it's own space and heat all around to get cooked properly.

- While threading meat, the skewers should be **pushed gently**. They should be woven through the tikka. This way there are less chances of meat slipping down.

- Pastes like raw papaya paste, ginger-garlic paste, onion paste, coriander paste or chilli paste should be made with as little water as possible.

- To keep the tikkas/ kebabs soft and succulent, **baste food** with some melted butter/oil or sometimes with the left over marinade. To baste, just pour the oil/ butter on the food that is being barbecued when it is a little more than half done.

- To check if meat is fully cooked, break it a little. If it breaks off easily, it is done, otherwise it needs to be cooked more.

- If the mutton is not of very good quality, you may **first pressure cook** the mutton and then marinate the cooked mutton and barbecue later at the time of serving .

Burrah Kebab

Mutton marinated in yogurt & vinegar, spiced with special royal cumin & pepper.

Serves 6   *Picture on cover*

½ kg Lamb chops
3 tbsp oil, 1¼ tsp salt

MARINADE
1 cup yogurt - hang in a muslin cloth for 30 minutes
1 tbsp kachri powder or 1 tbsp raw papaya paste (kaccha papita)- peel, deseed and grind a small piece of green papaya in a mixer
2 tbsp vinegar or lemon juice, 2 tbsp oil
2 tbsp ginger-garlic paste, 1½ tsp green chilli paste
2 tsp shah jeera (black cumin)
2 tsp tandoori masala, 1 tsp garam masala, 2 tsp freshly ground pepper

BASTING (FOR POURING ON THE KEBABS)
4 tbsp melted butter or oil

1. Wash and drain the chops. Pat them dry on a kitchen towel. Beat them with a belan to flatten them slightly.
2. Heat 3 tbsp oil in a pan. Add chops & stir fry for 10 minutes. Remove from fire.
3. Mix the ingredients of the marinade - curd, kachri powder, vinegar, 2 tbsp oil, ginger-garlic paste, green chilli paste, shah jeera, tandoori masala, garam masala, and pepper. Add mutton chops. Keep aside for 4 hours.
4. Add salt and keep for another 15 minutes.
5. Heat an electric oven at 180°C or a gas tandoor on gas for 15 minutes.
6. Place the well coated chops on a greased wire grill, rub them with the left over marinade.
7. Grill the chops for 15 minutes, turning once in between and basting the chops with oil or butter. Grill for another 10 minutes or till tender. You can check if the mutton is soft with a knife also.
8. Serve with dahi poodina chutney (see page 118) and mixed green relish (see page 121).

Note:
- Cover the tray beneath the wire rack or the skewers with aluminium foil to collect the drippings of the chops.
- The tenderizer (kachri powder or papaya paste is important to get soft kebabs. But do not marinade the chops with the tenderizer for too long (overnight) as the meat gets mushy on doing so. But give it 4 hours to soften.

Samarkand Boti

Boneless boti of lamb in fine paste of almonds & pistachios blended with rich spices.

Serves 6

½ kg (500 gm) mutton (boneless)
a few drops of tandoori red colour
1½ tsp lemon juice
1 tsp amchoor
1½" piece ginger & 8-10 flakes garlic - grind together to a paste

2ND MARINADE
2 tbsp almond (badam) paste- soak and peel 2 tbsp almonds and grind
2 tbsp pistachio (pista) paste - soak, peel and grind
1½ tbsp kachri powder or 1½ tbsp raw papaya paste (kaccha papita) - peel, deseed
and grind a small piece of raw papaya in a mixer
1 tsp shah jeera (black cumin seeds)
½ tsp ajwain (carom seeds)
¼ tsp grated jaiphal (nutmeg)
1 tsp salt, ½ tsp kala- namak (black salt)
1 tsp red chilli powder
2 tsp dhania powder, 3 tbsp oil

MASALA TO SPRINKLE (grind in a spice grinder or crush on a chakla-belan)
3 laung (cloves) , 1" piece dalchini (cinnamon)
seeds of 3 moti illaichi (brown cardamoms)
1 tsp bhuna shah jeera (roasted black cumin)

1. Cut the mutton into 2" cubes. Wash and pat dry the pieces. Prick them with a fork. Add colour and mix well. Add lemon juice, amchoor and ginger-garlic paste to the mutton cubes. Marinate for 1 hour.
2. Mix all the ingredients of second marinade except salt. Add this to the marinated mutton. Mix thoroughly and leave the mutton cubes soaked in this marinade for 3 - 4 hours in the refrigerator. Cover with a cling wrap/film.
3. Add salt 15 minutes before grilling. Heat the oven at 180°C. Oil and wipe the skewers or a greased wire rack of an oven. Thread 5-6 cubes of mutton on to each greased skewer, rub with the left over marinade or place the botis on a greased wire rack. Grill and cook for 20-25 minutes. Pour or drip melted butter on them to baste the botis.
4. Turn the skewer. Baste again with melted butter. Roast for 5 minutes more. Remove. Sprinkle with freshly ground masala and some lemon juice.
5. Serve hot along with til chutney (see page 119) and sirke waale pyaaz (see page 120) seasoned with salt, red chilli powder and lime juice.

Galouti Kebab

Delicious kebabs which melt in your mouth! Must give it a try.

Makes 15 kebabs

PRESSURE COOK TOGETHER
500 gm keema (lamb mince)
½ tsp garam masala
¼ tsp jaiphal (nutmeg) powder, ¼ tsp javetri (mace)
seeds of 3 moti illaichi, 2" stick dalchini (cinnamon)

OTHER INGREDIENTS
1½ tbsp kachri powder
¼ tsp mitha soda (soda-bi-carb)
2 onions - cut into slices, 2 tbsp ginger-garlic paste
1 egg white - separate egg yolk from egg white
4 tbsp besan (gram flour)
2 tbsp chopped coriander
1 tsp tandoori masala, ½ tsp garam masala, ½ tsp red chilli powder
1 tsp salt or to taste
5 tbsp melted butter, oil for frying

BATTER
1 egg, 2 tsp maida (plain flour)

1. Wash the mince in a strainer and press out excess water.
2. Put the mince in a cooker. Add ¼ tsp jaiphal, ¼ tsp javetri, seeds of 3 moti illaichi, 1" stick dalchini and 4 cups water. Give 5-6 whistles. Remove from fire. The keema should be cooked. After the pressure drops, if there is any water, dry out the water completely on fire.
3. Place boiled mince in a mixer blender. Churn till smooth. Keep aside.
4. Heat 1 cup oil in a kadhai and fry the sliced onions till golden brown. Remove from oil with a slotted spoon and grind to a brown paste.
5. Add the brown onion paste, ginger-garlic paste, kachri powder, 1 egg white, salt, chilli powder, tandoori masala and garam masala to the mince mixture. Mix to get a sticky consistency. Remove to a bowl.
6. Roast besan in a kadhai or pan on low heat till light golden and fragrant.
7. Add roasted besan and chopped coriander to the mince mixture. Add butter. Keep for 1 hour in the refrigerator. Shape mince into flat, 4" diameter tikkis.
8. Beat 1 egg and add 1 tsp maida to it. Dip the tikkis into the egg batter.
9. Shallow fry on low heat in 4 tbsp oil on a tawa or pan, till brown on both sides. Sprinkle some chaat masala and serve with onion rings mixed with some lemon juice and dahi poodina chutney. Serve hot.

Besani Mutton Seekh

Picture on page 57   *Serves 6-8*

½ kg (500 gm) mutton mince - (keema)
4 green chillies - deseeded and finely chopped
2 tbsp coriander - finely chopped
2 tbsp mint - finely chopped

1 ST MARINADE
1 big onion - sliced and deep fried to a golden colour
½ tsp haldi, 1 tsp red chilli powder, 1 tsp salt, 2 tbsp oil
1 tbsp kachri powder or 1 tbsp raw papaya paste (kacha papita) - peel, deseed and
grind a small piece of raw papaya in a mixer
½ tsp mitha soda (soda-bi-carbonate)
4 tbsp besan - roasted on a tawa for a minute till fragrant

GRIND TO A FINE PASTE
½ cup cashewnuts (kaju)
1 tbsp almonds - blanch (soak in hot water and peel)
5" piece of fresh coconut- remove the brown skin and grate (6 tbsp)
2 tsp dhania powder (coriander powder)
4 laung (cloves), 3 sticks dalchini (cinnamon), 1 tsp shah jeera (black cumin seeds)

1. Wash mince in a strainer and press to squeeze out all the excess water. Grind it in a grinder to a paste. Add kachri powder or papaya paste and mitha soda.
2. Mix fried onions, chilli powder, haldi, oil & salt to mince. Keep aside for 1 hour.
3. Grind cashewnuts, almonds, coconut, coriander powder and whole spices in a mixer to a fine paste with 4 tbsp water. Keep aside.
4. Add green chillies, coriander, mint and the prepared cashew paste to the mince. Leave aside for 3 hours.
5. At the time of serving, add roasted besan. Mix well.
6. Heat an oven at 180°C or a gas tandoor on gas at moderate flame.
7. Take a big ball of the mince mixture and hold a well greased hot skewer carefully in the other hand. Press the mince onto the hot skewer carefully. The mince will immediately stick to the hot skewer. If the skewers are cold the mince will not stick. Make one big seekh on the skewer. Repeat with the left over mince on all the other skewers.
8. Place the skewers in the hot oven or tandoor. Cook for 15-20 minutes or till done. Baste with 4 tbsp oil in between. Grill for another 5 minutes.
9. Remove the seekh gently from the skewer. Cut each into 1" pieces diagonally to serve. Sprinkle chaat masala and serve hot.

Dhania Adrak Champe

For those who like ginger, these chops will be irresistible. Spinach adds an authentic touch.

Serves 6

½ kg Lamb chops
4 tbsp oil, 1 tsp salt

MARINADE
1 cup yogurt - hang is a muslin cloth for ½ hour
1 tbsp vinegar or lemon juice
1½" piece ginger - finely grated
1 tbsp oil, ½ tsp pepper

GRIND TO A PASTE (GREEN PASTE)
1 tbsp kachri powder or 1 tbsp raw papaya paste (kacha papita) - peel, deseed and grind a small piece of raw papaya in a mixer
½ tsp mitha soda (soda-bi-carbonate)
10 fresh spinach leaves
2" piece ginger, 3 tsp green coriander, 4 green chillies

BASTING (POURING ON THE KEBABS)
4 tbsp melted butter or oil

1. Wash and drain the chops. Pat them dry on a kitchen towel. Beat them with a belan to flatten them. Prick them with a fork.
2. Heat 4 tbsp oil in a pan. Add chops. Stir fry for 5-10 minutes. Remove from fire.
3. Grind raw papaya, mitha soda, spinach leaves, ginger, coriander & green chillies to a paste.
4. Mix the ingredients of the marinade - curd, vinegar, ginger, pepper, 1 tbsp oil and the ground green paste. Add fried mutton chops. Keep aside for 4 hours.
5. Add salt and keep for another 15 minutes.
6. Heat an electric oven at 180°C or a gas tandoor on gas at moderate flame.
7. Place the well coated chops on a greased wire rack or grill, rub them with the left over marinade.
8. Grill the chops for 15 minutes, turning once in between and basting (pour) the chops with oil or butter. Grill for another 10 minutes or till tender.
9. Serve with poodina chutney and peanut cabbage relish (see page 119, 121).

Note:

- If the meat is not of very good quality, you may first pressure cook the mutton and then barbecue later along with the marinade.

Boti Din Raat

Delicious mutton kebabs served in boiled eggs.

Picture on page 47   *Serves 8-10*

250 gms mutton (boneless) - cut into 1" pieces

1ST MARINADE
1 tbsp lemon juice
3 tbsp ginger-garlic paste

2ND MARINADE
¼ tsp saffron (kesar), ½ tsp milk
1 cup thick curd - tie in a muslin cloth & hang for 1 hour
1 tbsp kachri powder or 1 tbsp raw papaya paste (kachha papita) - peel, deseed
and grind a small piece of raw papaya in a mixer
¼ tsp soda-bicarbonate (mitha soda)
2 onions - cut into slices, deep fried till golden and ground to a paste
½ tsp green cardamom powder (chhoti illaichi)
1 tsp salt
1 tsp pepper powder

TO SERVE
5 hard boiled eggs - halved and egg yolk separated from egg white

1. Soak the kesar in ½ tsp milk for a few minutes.
2. Cut the mutton into 1" cubes. Wash and pat dry the pieces. Prick them with a fork. Mix lemon juice and ginger-garlic paste with the mutton cubes. Keep aside for half an hour.
3. Mix all the ingredients of 2nd marinade- kesar, curd, papaya paste or kachri powder, mitha soda, fried onion paste, chhoti illaichi, salt and pepper.
4. Add marinated mutton to the second marinade mixture. Mix thoroughly. Let the mutton marinate in this for atleast 4 hours or even more in the refrigerator.
5. To cook the botis, remove from fridge and let them come to room temperature. Heat an electric oven at 150°C or a gas tandoor on gas at moderate flame. Thread 5 to 6 pieces of mutton onto each greased skewer or place the botis on a greased wire rack of the oven. Rub with the left over marinade
6. Grill for 15- 20 minutes turning them 2 to 3 times inbetween. When slightly dry, spoon or brush some (about 2 tbsp) oil on them. Cook for another 10 minutes or till done. Remove the tikkas from the skewer.
7. Hard boil the eggs. Cool, peel and cut into half widthwise. Remove the egg yolk from the egg white. Put a piece of tikka in the hollowed egg.

contd...

8. Sprinkle garam masala. Serve hot with dahi-poodina chutney and onion rings seasoned with salt, red chilli powder and lime juice.

Note:

- An **interesting side dish** from the boiled egg yolks to be served along:
  Chop the 5 boiled egg yolks coarsely and mix lightly with 1 finely chopped onion, 2 chopped green chillies, 1 tbsp chopped coriander and 1 tsp oil. Sprinkle with salt and pepper. Add 1 tbsp lemon juice. Serve.

- Grilling or roasting should be done on constant moderate heat, otherwise it toughens the protein of the meat, making the kebabs shrink and turn hard.
- Always grease the wire rack or grill nicely with oil to avoid the kebabs sticking to the grill.
- If the meat is not of very good quality, you may first pressure cook the mutton and then barbecue later along with the marinade.

Mutton & Tomato Kebabs

Picture on facing page   Serves 5 - 6

PRESSURE COOK TOGETHER
500 gm keema (lamb mince)
½ tsp garam masala
seeds of 3 moti illaichi, 2" stick dalchini (cinnamon)
¼ tsp salt

OTHER INGREDIENTS
2 medium sized onions
1 tbsp kachri powder or 1 tbsp raw papaya paste (green papita) - peel, deseed and grind a small piece of raw papaya in a mixer
3-4 flakes garlic, 1 dry red chilli - broken into pieces
1½ tsp garam masala, 1 tsp lemon juice, 1½ tbsp oil
¼ tsp red chilli powder, ½ tsp salt or to taste
2½ tbsp mint leaves or fresh coriander - finely chopped
4 small tomatoes - each cut into 4 and pulp removed

BASTING
2 tbsp melted butter or oil

1. Place the mince in a strainer. Wash and squeeze out excess water.
2. In a cooker add seeds of 3 moti illaichi, 2" stick dalchini, salt and 4 cups water. Give 5 whistles. Remove from fire. The keema should be cooked. After the pressure drops, if there is any water in the cooker, dry out the water completely on fire.
3. Place the boiled mince in a mixer blender. Churn till smooth.
4. Finely chop 1 onion and cut the remaining onion into 4 big pieces.
5. Heat 1 tbsp oil in a kadhai and fry the chopped onion till golden brown. Remove from oil with a slotted spoon.
6. Place the mince in a mixer. Add the fried onion, garlic, dry red chilli, garam masala, lemon juice, 1½ tbsp oil, chilli powder and salt. Grind to get a sticky consistency. Remove to a bowl. Add chopped mint leaves or fresh coriander.
7. Make 10-15 marble sized balls with well greased hands.
8. Thread a mince ball, then a piece of tomato and lastly onion on to each skewer. Repeat.
9. Grill under a hot grill at 180° C for 15 minutes, turning them 2 or 3 times. Baste with melted butter or oil on them. Cook for another 10 minutes or till done. Sprinkle some chaat masala and some lemon juice. Serve with poodina chutney.

Boti Din Raat : Recipe on page 44, Dal makhani : Recipe on page 123
Til chutney : Recipe on page 119, Mutton & Tomato Kebabs ➤

Masala Chops

Delicious chops with an impressive look and unique taste!

Picture on page 37   *Serves 6*

½ kg lamb chops (preferably big size chops), 3 tbsp oil
2 tsp salt

MARINADE
1½ cups yogurt- hang for ½ hour in a muslin cloth
1 tbsp kachri powder or 1 tbsp raw papaya paste (green papita) - peel, deseed and grind a small piece of raw papaya in a mixer
1 tbsp lemon juice or vinegar
5 tsp curry powder (MDH)
2 tsp ajwain (carom seeds)
1 tsp tandoori masala or barbecue masala
1 tsp haldi
3 tsp oil

GRIND TO A FINE GREEN PASTE
2" piece ginger, 10 flakes garlic
5 green chillies, 2 tbsp roughly chopped green coriander

BASTING (POURING OIL IN BETWEEN GRILLING)
2 tbsp melted butter or oil

1. Wash and drain the chops. Pat them dry on a clean kitchen towel. Beat them with a meat mallet or belan to flatten them. Prick them with a fork.
2. Heat 3 tbsp oil in a pan. Add the chops and stir fry for 5-10 minutes. Remove from fire.
3. Mix in the ingredients of marinade - yoghurt, lemon juice, curry powder, ajwain, tandoori masala, kachri powder, haldi, oil and the ground green paste also.
   Add fried mutton chops. Keep aside for atleast 4 hours or even more in the refrigerator.
4. Just 15 minutes before putting in the oven, add salt and keep for another 15 minutes outside so that they come to room temperature.
5. Heat an electric oven at 150°C or a gas tandoor on gas at low moderate flame.
6. Place well coated chops on a greased grill. Pat chops with the remaining marinade.
7. Grill the chops for 20 minutes, turning once in between and basting (pouring) the chops with oil or butter. Grill for another 10 minutes or till tender. You can check if the mutton is soft with a knife also.
8. Sprinkle chaat masala and serve with poodina chutney and onion rings.

Kebab Rukha Seekh Par

Unique combination of mutton, zucchini and rice.

Serves 6

½ kg mutton mince (keema), 3 moti illaichi, 1" stick dalchini, ½ tsp salt

1ST MARINADE
1½ tbsp kachri powder or 1½ tbsp raw papaya paste (papita) - peel, deseed and grind a small piece of raw papaya in a mixer, ½ tbsp amchoor, 2 tsp oil

GRIND TO A PASTE
2 green chillies, 1 tsp basil or tulsi, 1 tbsp coriander and 1 tsp roasted jeera (cumin)

2ND MARINADE
¾ cup boiled rice, 1 cup zucchini (tori) - peeled and finely sliced
2 tbsp coriander chopped, 1 tsp salt, 3 tbsp maida (plain flour)
1 tsp oil, a pinch of tandoori colour - optional
1 egg white

1. Place the mince in a strainer. Wash and squeeze out excess water.
2. In a cooker add mince, seeds of 3 moti illaichi, 1" stick dalchini, salt and 4 cups water. Give 3-4 whistles. Remove from fire. The keema should be cooked. After the pressure drops, if there is any water left, dry it out completely on fire.
3. Place the boiled mince in a mixer blender. Churn till smooth.
4. Marinate the mutton mince with the 1st marinade- papaya paste, amchoor, oil and the ground paste of green chillies, coriander, jeera and tulsi leaves. Leave aside for 1 hour.
5. Deep fry tori till all the water has evaporated. Add all ingredients of 2nd marinade to the fried tori except egg- boiled rice, coriander, oil, colour, maida and salt.
6. Grind marinated tori in grinder. Add marinated mince to the tori mixture. Marinate for 3 hours.
7. Beat the egg and add it to the minced tori and mutton mixture.
8. Heat an oven at 180°C or gas tandoor on gas at moderate flame with skewers.
9. Take a big ball of the mince and hold a hot skewer carefully in the other hand. Press the mince on to a skewer. The mince will immediately stick to the skewer.
10. Make 1 big seekh on the skewer. Repeat with left over mince on all other skewers.
11. Place the skewers in the hot oven or tandoor. Cook for 20 minutes or till done, rotating the skewers and basting with some oil in between. When the seekhs get cooked, gently remove the kebab from the skewers with the help of a cloth.
12. Shallow fry the prepared seekh kebabs on non stick pan in 1-2 tbsp oil till golden brown. Serve with chilli garlic chutney (see page 119) and sirke waale pyaaz.

Kakori Kebab

Situated on the banks of the Gomti river, Kakori is a place well known for its revolutionaries and for it's kebabs. The famous Kakori kebabs originated here.

Serves 8

500 gm mutton keema (lamb mince)

MARINADE
2 onions - cut into slices, deep fried till golden and ground to a paste
2-3 green chillies - very finely chopped
seeds of 3-4 chhoti illaichi (green cardamoms) - crushed
seeds of 1 moti illaichi (black cardamoms) - crushed
½ tsp grated jaiphal (nutmeg)
¼ tsp mitha soda (soda-bi-carb)
½ tsp freshly ground saboot kali mirch (black peppercorns)
2-3 laung (cloves)
2 tbsp oil
2 eggs
4 tbsp powdered bhuna channas (roasted bengal gram flour)
1 tsp salt

BASTING (pouring in-between grilling)
4 tbsp melted butter or oil

1. Grind the mince twice till smooth.
2. Mix the ingredients of the marinade. Rub well into the mince. The process of rubbing in is important as all the ingredients have to blend well with the mince. Leave aside for 4 hours in the refrigerator.
3. Remove the mince from the fridge a little before serving time, so that the mince comes to room temperature before you put them in the oven or tandoor.
4. At serving time, oil and wipe the skewers. Heat an electric oven at 180°C or a gas tandoor on gas at moderate flame.
5. Press mince into sausage-shaped kebabs directly onto the greased skewers. Make one long kebab on the skewer.
6. Put the skewers into the hot oven or tandoor and cook for 8 minutes. Pour or drip melted butter on them to baste the kebabs.
7. Turn the skewer. Baste again with melted butter. Roast for 5 minutes more.
8. Serve with chutney, onion rings and lemon. Sprinkle chaat masala on the kebabs and onions. Serve hot with chilli garlic chutney.

Note: Pastes like raw papaya paste, ginger-garlic paste or onion paste should be made with as little water as possible while preparing tikkas and kebabs.

Boti Kebab

Mutton on skewers.

Serves 6

1ST MARINADE
½ kg (500) gm mutton - cut into 2" pieces
a few drops of tandoori red colour
1 tsp lemon juice, 1 tsp amchoor
1½" piece ginger & 8-10 flakes garlic - ground together to a paste

2ND MARINADE
1 cup thick curd - tie in a muslin cloth and hang for 1 hour
1 tbsp kachri powder or 1 tbsp raw papaya paste (green papita) - peel, deseed and
grind a small piece of raw papaya in a mixer
1 tsp shah jeera (black cumin seeds)
½ to 1 tsp ajwain (carom seeds)
¼ tsp grated jaiphal (nutmeg)
1¼ tsp salt, ½ tsp black salt, 1 tsp red chilli powder, 2 tsp dhania powder
2 tsp vinegar, 2 tbsp oil

MASALA TO SPRINKLE (grind in a spice grinder or crush on a chakla-belan)
3 laung (cloves), 1" piece dalchini (cinnamon)
seeds of 3 moti illaichi (brown cardamoms)
1 tsp bhuna shah jeere (roasted black cumin)
2 tbsp kasoori methi (dried fenugreek leaves)

1. Cut mutton into 2" cubes. Wash and pat dry the pieces. Prick them with a fork. Add the colouring on it and mix well. Mix lemon juice and amchoor with the ginger-garlic paste and mix this paste with the mutton cubes. Keep aside for half an hour.

2. Mix all the ingredients of second marinade. Add this to the marinated mutton. Mix thoroughly and leave the mutton cubes soaked in this marinade for 3 to 4 hours in the refrigerator.

3. To cook the botis, thread 5 to 6 cubes of mutton on to each skewer, rub with the left over marinade.

4. Cook in a oven at 180°C for 15 to 20 minutes, turning them 2 or 3 times. When slightly dry, spoon or brush some oil on them. Cook till done. You can check if the mutton is soft with a knife also. Sprinkle with freshly ground masala and some lemon juice.

5. Serve hot on the skewers along with hari chutney and sliced onions seasoned with salt, red chilli powder and lemon juice.

Shami Kebab

An all time favourite kebab!

Makes 15 kebabs

PRESSURE COOK TOGETHER
½ kg mutton mince (keema)
¼ cup channa dal - soaked in warm water for 20-30 minutes and drained
1 onion - sliced
10 flakes garlic - chopped
2" piece ginger - chopped
2 tsp saboot dhania (coriander seeds)
1 tsp jeera (cumin seeds)
3- 4 laung (cloves)
2 chhoti illaichi (green cardamoms)
2 moti illaichi (brown cardamoms)
½" stick dalchini (cinnamon)
1 tej patta (bay leaf)
4-5 saboot kali mirch (peppercorns)
2-3 dry, whole red chillies
salt to taste
2 tbsp oil
1 cup water

1. Wash the mince in a strainer and press well to drain out the water well through the strainer.
2. Add all the ingredients to the mince and pressure cook to give 2 whistles. Keep on low flame for 2 minutes. Remove from fire.
3. When the pressure drops, uncover the pressure cooker. If there is any water left, keep the cooker on fire to dry the water. (If the mince is wet, the kebabs will break while frying).
4. Dry grind the well dried minced meat either on a stone grinder or in a mixer till smooth without adding any water while grinding. (Discard hard residue of moti illaichi and bay leaf).
5. To prepare kebabs, make balls. Flatten them to get thick, round 2½" diameter tikkis.
6. Shallow fry in a little oil in a non stick tawa on medium heat, till brown.
7. Sprinkle chaat masala and serve hot with dahi poodina chutney (*see page- 118*) and mixed green relish (*see page-121*).

Lamb Tikka Masala

Dry mutton tikka coated with thick masala.

Serves 4   *Picture on page 127*

½ kg cooked mutton tikka
(prepare mutton tikka as given (boti din raat) on page 44)

MASALA
2 tbsp oil
¼ tsp sarson (mustard seeds), ½ tsp kalonji (black onion seeds)
1 onion - sliced
2 tomatoes - chopped
2 green chillies - finely chopped
½ cup coconut milk, see note
½ tsp salt, or to taste
2 tbsp poodina (mint leaves) - finely chopped
2 tbsp coriander - finely chopped
1½ tbsp lemon juice
½ tsp garam masala

1. Prepare boti tikka as given on page 44 till step 6. Keep tikka aside.
2. For the masala, heat 2 tbsp oil. Add sarson and kalonji.
3. Wait for a minute. Add onion and garlic. Saute over medium heat until onions turn golden brown.
4. Add tomatoes and chopped green chillies. Cook till oil separates.
5. Add coconut milk and salt. Bring to a boil, stirring continuously. Lower heat and cook for 5-10 minutes or until masala turns thick.
6. At the time of serving, remove the cooked mutton tikka from the skewers and add to the masala.
7. Add chopped mint, coriander, lemon juice and garam masala.
8. Serve hot with dahi poodina chutney and mixed green salad.

Note: Ready made coconut milk powder is available. For preparing coconut milk with powder - mix ¼ cup coconut milk powder (maggi) with ½ cup water.

To make fresh coconut milk, grate ½ of a fresh coconut and put 1 cup hot water on it. Leave aside for 15 minutes. Blend in a mixer and strain to get coconut milk. Use as required.

Kulfi Kebab

Serves 6

½ kg mutton (boneless) - cut into 1" strips lengthwise
4 tbsp oil , 1 tej patta (bay leaf), 1 laung (clove)
¼ tsp mitha soda (soda-bi-carb), 2 tbsp oil

GRIND TOGETHER TO A PASTE

1 tbsp kachri powder or 1 tbsp raw papaya paste (green papita) - peel, deseed and
grind a small piece of raw papaya in a mixer
1½ tbsp ginger, 2 green chillies
1 onion - sliced and deep fried
2 tbsp walnuts (akhrot), 2 khajoor (dates) - chopped finely, 2 tsp nyoze (pine nuts)
1 tsp garam masala, 2 tsp khus- khus (poppy seeds)
2 tsp roasted shah jeera (black cumin)
1 tsp chilli powder, 1 tsp salt, 2 tbsp oil

BATTER

1 cup yogurt - hang in a muslin cloth for 30 minutes
1 tsp green chilli paste, 3 tbsp almond paste (blanch, peel and grind almonds)
¼ tsp garam masala, 4 tbsp maida (plain flour)
1 egg white, ½ tsp salt

BASTING (POURING IN BETWEEN GRILLING)- 3 tbsp oil

1. Wash the tikkas. Pat dry. Prick them with a fork.
2. In a pressure cooker put the mutton strips, tej patta, laung, oil, salt, mitha soda
    and 2 cups water. Boil. Give 3 whistles & cook for 5 minutes. Remove & drain.
3. Grind ginger, fried onion, green chilli, walnuts, dates, shah jeera and khus-
    khus in a grinder. Keep paste aside.
4. Mix garam masala, chilli powder and 2 tbsp oil to the paste, except salt.
5. Add mutton strips to the mixture. Leave aside for 6 hours.
6. Heat 4 tbsp oil in a pan. Add marinated mutton strips and salt. Fry on high flame
    for 5-10 minutes. Remove from fire.
7. Mix all the ingredients of the batter in a shallow flat bowl. Add the marinated
    mutton to it.
8. Heat an electric oven at 180°C or a gas tandoor on gas at moderate flame.
9. Place the well coated tikkas on a greased wire rack or grill, rub them with the left
    over marinade.
10. Grill the tikkas for 15-20 minutes, turning them 2 or 3 times. When slightly dry,
    spoon or brush some oil on them. Cook for another 5 minutes or till tender. You
    can check if the mutton is soft with a knife also. Sprinkle lemon juice. Serve.

Tikka Achaari

Pickle flavoured mutton, simply irresistible!

Serves 6

½ kg (500) gm mutton - cut into 2" pieces
4 tbsp oil for basting (pouring on the tikkas inbetween grilling)

1ST MARINADE
a few drops of tandoori red colour
1 tsp lemon juice, 1 tsp amchoor
1½" piece ginger & 8-10 flakes garlic - grind to a paste together (1½ tbsp)

2ND MARINADE
1 cup thick curd - tie in a muslin cloth and hang for 1 hour
1 tbsp kachri powder or 1 tbsp raw papaya paste (green papita) - peel, deseed and
grind a small piece of raw papaya in a mixer
1 onion- sliced, fried till golden and ground to a paste
1¼ tsp salt, 1 tsp red chilli powder, 2 tbsp oil

ACHAARI MASALA
2 tsp saunf (fennel)
1 tsp rai (mustard seeds), 1 tsp jeera (cumin seeds)
a pinch of methi daana (fenugreek seeds)
½ tsp kalonji (onion seeds)

1. Cut the mutton into 2" cubes. Wash and pat dry the pieces. Prick them with a fork. Add the colour to it and mix well.
2. Mix lemon juice, amchoor and the ginger-garlic paste. Mix this paste with the mutton cubes. Keep aside for half an hour.
3. Collect all seeds of the achaari masala together.
4. Mix all the ingredients of second marinade with the collected achaari masala in a bowl. Add this to the marinated mutton. Mix thoroughly and leave the mutton cubes soaked in this marinade for atleast 3 to 4 hours or even more in the refrigerator.
5. To cook the botis, remove from fridge and let them come to room temperature. Thread 5 to 6 cubes of mutton on to each skewer, rub with the left over marinade.
6. Grill in a hot oven at 150°C or in a gas tandoor on low moderate flame for 20 minutes, turning them 2 or 3 times in between.
7. When the coating is slightly dry, baste with oil (pour some oil on them). Cook for another 10 minutes or till done. Sprinkle with freshly ground pepper and some lemon juice. Serve hot with poodina chutney and sirke waale pyaaz.

Mutton Egg nets Kebab

Mixture of minced mutton and eggs. Extra soft kebab with an impressive look.

Picture on facing page   *Serves 6 - 8*

PRESSURE COOK TOGETHER
500 gm keema (lamb mince)
seeds of 3 moti illaichi (brown cardamom)
2" stick dalchini (cinnamon)
¼ tsp salt, ½ tsp garam masala

GRIND TO A PASTE
2 red, yellow or green capsicum - chopped coarsely
1 tbsp kachri powder or 1 tbsp raw papaya paste (papita) - peel, deseed and grind
a small piece of raw papaya in a mixer, optional, ½ tsp mitha soda
1 tsp chilli powder
2 tsp saboot dhania (coriander seeds), 2 tsp jeera (cumin seeds)
1" piece ginger, 5-6 flakes garlic
2 tbsp thick cream, 2 eggs
¾ tsp salt, ½ tsp pepper

OTHER INGREDIENTS
2 tsp maida, 4 tbsp oil for frying

1. Place the mince in a strainer. Wash and squeeze out excess water.
2. In a cooker add seeds of 3 moti illaichi, dalchini, salt, garam masala and 4 cups water. Give 5-6 whistles. Remove from fire. The keema should be cooked. After the pressure drops, if there is any water, dry out the water completely on fire.
3. Place the boiled mince in a mixer blender. Churn till smooth.
4. Grind the capsicum, chilli powder, coriander seeds, jeera, ginger, garlic, cream, eggs, salt and pepper in a blender. Blend till smooth. Strain through a strainer. Reserve the capsicum liquid. To the mixture without the liquid in the strainer, add minced lamb.
5. Blend mince again to get a sticky consistency. Remove to a bowl.
6. Shape mince into flat tikkis with greased hands. Keep them in the fridge for 30 minutes.
7. Heat a non stick pan with 4 tbsp oil.
8. Beat the reserved capsicum liquid, add maida to it. Dip the tikkis in this batter.
9. Shallow fry on medium heat in 4 tbsp oil till light golden on both sides. Keep on low heat till the mince gets cooked properly and it turns brown.
10. Sprinkle some chaat masala. Serve with chilli garlic chutney (see page 119).

Besani Mutton Seekh : Recipe on page 42, Mutton Egg nets Kebabs ➤

Hing Tikka

Pre-cooked meat kebabs are delicious and great time savers. Do try this recipe.

Serves 6

½ kg (500) gm mutton (boneless) - cut into 2" pieces
½ tsp saboot kali mirch (black peppercorns)
½ tsp jaiphal (nutmeg) powder, ¼ tsp javetri (mace) powder
1 tej patta (bay leaf), 1 laung (clove)
¼ tsp mitha soda (soda-bi-carb), 2 tbsp oil
½ tsp haldi (turmeric powder), 1 tsp salt

1ST MARINADE
3 tbsp oil, ½ tsp hing (asafoetida)

2ND MARINADE
1 cup yogurt - hang in a muslin cloth for ½ hour
1 tbsp kachri powder or 1 tbsp raw papaya paste (green papita) - peel, deseed and
grind a small piece of raw papaya in a mixer
1½ tsp bhuna jeera powder (ground roasted cumin)
1½ tsp dhania powder (coriander)
½ tsp ginger dry powder (optional), 1 tsp amchoor (raw mango powder)
2 tbsp oil

BASTING (POURING ON THE TIKKAS)
2 tbsp oil mixed with ½ tsp hing

1. Wash the tikkas. Pat dry. Prick them with a fork.
2. In a pressure cooker put the mutton pieces, kali mirch, javetri, jaiphal, tej patta, laung, oil, salt and 2 cups water. Boil. Give 3 whistle and cook for 5 minutes. Remove from fire and drain.
3. Heat 3 tbsp oil in a pan, fry the tikkas. Add hing (1st marinade). Fry till light brown, keep aside and cool.
4. Mix all ingredients of 2nd marinade. Soak the tikkas in this marinade for two hours or till required for serving.
5. Heat an electric oven at 180°C or a gas tandoor on gas at moderate flame.
6. Place the well coated kebabs on a greased wire rack or grill, rub them with the left over marinade.
7. Grill the kebabs for 15 minutes, turning once in between. When slightly dry, baste with oil mixed with hing. Grill for another 5 minutes or till tender. You can check if the mutton is cooked and soft by inserting a knife.
8. Sprinkle lemon juice. Serve hot with chilli garlic chutney (see page 119).

Shikampuri Kebab

Mince kebabs with a filling of hard boiled egg whites flavoured with mint and coriander.

Makes 15 kebabs

PRESSURE COOK TOGETHER
500 gms mutton mince (keema)
¼ cup channa dal (split gram)
10 flakes garlic
1 tsp shah jeera (black cumin seeds)
3-4 chhoti illaichi (green cardamoms)
2" stick dalchini (cinnamon)
4 laung (cloves)
2 tbsp oil

OTHER INGREDIENTS
¼ cup almonds - blanched (soaked in water) and peeled
2" piece of fresh coconut - remove the brown skin and grate
juice of ½ lemon (1 tbsp)
1 tsp salt or to taste, 1 tsp red chilli powder (degi mirch), ¼ tsp haldi
1 egg

FILLING
1 egg - hard boiled, discard yolk
½ of a small onion - chopped very finely
2 -3 green chillies - finely chopped
¼ tsp salt, ½ tsp garam masala
2 tbsp finely chopped mint (poodina), 2 tbsp finely chopped coriander

1. In a cooker add all ingredients with the mince. Add 1 cup water and give 5-6 whistles. Remove from fire. The keema and dal should be cooked. After the pressure drops, if there is any water in the cooker, dry out the water completely on fire.
2. To the keema, add the blanched almonds and grated coconut and bhuno for 2-3 minutes over medium heat. Remove from fire and cool.
3. Add lemon juice, salt, red chilli powder, haldi and egg to the keema.
4. Grind keema to a fine paste. Make 15 balls of the mince.
5. For the filling, divide boiled egg into two and remove the yolk. Chop white finely. Mix in chopped onion, green chillies, salt, garam masala, mint and coriander.
6. Flatten the mince balls and stuff a little filling. Smoothen out kebabs with wet hands. Deep fry to a rich brown colour.
7. Serve with dahi poodina chutney (see page 118) and onion rings.

Tikka Kandhari

Serves 6

1ST MARINADE
½ kg (500) gm mutton - cut into 2" pieces
a few drops of tandoori red colour
1 tsp lemon juice, 1 tsp amchoor
2 tbsp ginger-garlic paste

2ND MARINADE
½ cup thick curd - tie into a muslin cloth and hang for 1 hour
½ cup thick cream
1 tbsp kachri powder or 1 tbsp raw papaya paste (green papita) - peel, deseed and
grind a small piece of raw papaya in a mixer
½ to 1 tsp ajwain (carom seeds)
1 tsp chhoti illaichi (green cardamom) - crushed
1¼ tsp salt, ½ tsp black pepper, 1 tsp red chilli powder
2 tsp dhania powder, 1 tsp garam masala
3 tsp oil

TO SPRINKLE
½ tsp amchoor powder or lemon juice

BASTING (POURING ON THE TIKKAS) - 2 tbsp oil

1. Cut the mutton into 2" cubes. Wash and pat dry the pieces. Prick them with a fork. Add the colour on it and mix well. Mix lemon juice and amchoor with the ginger-garlic paste and mix this paste with the mutton cubes. Keep aside for half an hour.
2. Mix all the ingredients of second marinade. Add this to the marinated mutton. Mix thoroughly and leave the mutton cubes soaked in this marinade for 3-4 hours in the refrigerator.
3. Heat an electric oven at 180°C or a gas tandoor on gas at moderate flame.
4. Place the well coated tikkas on a greased wire rack or grill, rub them with the left over marinade.
5. Grill the tikkas for 15-20 minutes, turning once in between. When slightly dry, baste with some oil on them. Cook for another 5 minutes or till tender. You can check if the mutton is soft with a knife also. Sprinkle some amchoor or lemon juice.
6. Serve hot with chilli garlic chutney (see page 119) and khatti arbi ka salad (see page 120) or sliced onions seasoned with salt, red chilli powder & lemon juice.

Mutton Seekh

Succulent cocktail kebabs of lamb mince.

Serves 4- 6

½ kg lamb mince (keema)
2 onions - sliced, deep fried to a crisp brown colour and crushed
2 tsp ginger-garlic paste
2 tsp kaaju and 2 tsp khus khus(poppy seeds) - soak together for 15 minutes in a
little warm water and grind to a fine paste
1 tsp garam masala powder or tandoori masala
1 tbsp kachri powder or 1 tbsp raw papaya paste (green papita) - peel, deseed and
grind a small piece of raw papaya in a mixer
2 tsp thick cream or malai
salt to taste

DRY MASALA (MIX TOGETHER) TO SPRINKLE ON TOP
1 tsp salt, ½ tsp kala namak (rock salt)
½ tsp roasted jeera powder(bhuna jeera)
¼ tsp red chilli powder
¼ tsp citric powder

BASTING (pouring on the kebabs) - 2 tbsp melted butter

1. Wash the mince in a strainer and gently press to squeeze out all the water. Grind in a grinder to make it fine.
2. Mix all ingredients- onions, ginger-garlic paste, kaju-khus khus paste, garam masala, papaya paste, cream and salt to the mince and knead well. Keep aside for 1 hour.
3. Heat the electric oven with greased skewers at 180°C.
4. Take a big ball of the mince mixture and hold a hot skewer carefully in the other hand. Press the mince on to the skewer. The mince will immediately stick to the skewer.
5. Make another seekh on the same skewer, leaving a gap of 2". Repeat with the left over mince on all the other skewers.
6. Place the skewers in the hot oven. Cook for 10-15 minutes, rotating the skewers and basting with melted butter in between. Cook for another 5 minutes. When cooked, gently remove the kebab from the skewers with the help of a cloth.
7. Shallow fry the seekh kebabs on non stick pan or tawa in 1-2 tbsp oil till golden brown.
8. Mix all masalas of the dry masala and keep aside. To serve kebabs, sprinkle some dry masala and lemon juice on the hot kebabs.

Minty Kebabs

Makes 15 kebabs

PRESSURE COOK TOGETHER
½ kg mutton mince (keema)
¼ cup channa dal - soaked & drained
1 onion - sliced
10 flakes garlic - chopped, 2" piece ginger - chopped
2 tsp saboot dhania (coriander seeds)
1 tsp jeera (cumin seeds)
3-4 laung (cloves)
2 chhoti illaichi (green cardamoms)
2 moti illaichi (brown cardamoms)
½" stick dalchini (cinnamon), 1 bay leaf (tej patta)
4-5 saboot kali mirch (peppercorns)
2-3 dry, whole red chillies
salt to taste, 2 tbsp oil
½ cup water

MINTY FILLING (MIX TOGETHER)
1 onion - finely chopped
1 tbsp chopped poodina, 1 tbsp chopped hara dhania
2 green chillies - finely chopped

1. Wash the mince and drain out the water well through a strainer. Press well to squeeze out all the water.
2. Add all the ingredients to the mince and pressure cook to give 2 whistles. Keep on low flame for 2 minutes. Remove from fire.
3. When the pressure drops, uncover the pressure cooker. If there is any water left, keep the cooker on fire to dry the water. (If the mince is wet, the kebabs will break while frying).
4. Dry grind the well dried minced meat either on a stone grinder or in a mixer till smooth without adding any water while grinding. (Discard hard residue of moti illaichi and bay leaf)
5. To prepare the kebabs, make 2 tiny balls. Flatten both and sandwich them together with a teaspoon of the filling mixture. Press gently to stick together.
6. Shallow fry in a little oil in a non stick tawa on medium heat, till brown.
7. Serve with poodina chutney (see page-119) and mixed green relish (see page-121).

Note: When you cook the tikkas in the oven, place a drip tray under the wire rack on which the tikkas are placed, to collect the drippings.

Boti Ka Salad

Mutton tikka salad in a clove flavoured yogurt dressing

Serves 4

½ kg cooked mutton tikka
(prepare mutton tikka as given (boti din raat) on page 44)

SALAD
2 onions - cut into eight pieces and separated
2 tomatoes - cut into eight and deseed
2 green chillies - slit lengthwise, deseed and then chop

DRESSING
1 cup yogurt - hang in muslin cloth for ½ hour
¼ cup mint leaves - chopped finely
2 tbsp lemon juice
3- 4 clove (laung) - powdered (½ tsp)
½ tsp freshly ground pepper
½ tsp salt

1. Prepare boti kebab till step-6 as given on page 44.
2. For the dressing, whisk the hung yogurt in a bowl. Add chopped mint leaves, lemon juice, powdered laung, pepper and salt. Mix well. Add more seasoning according to taste.
3. Mix together, the prepared boti kebab and the onions, tomatoes, green chillies in a bowl.
4. Pour the yogurt dressing on the mixed vegetable and mutton botis. Toss well.
5. Serve chilled with chilli garlic chutney (see page 119) and roasted papad.

Note: Chicken tikka salad can also be prepared in the same way. Prepare chicken tikka as given on page 24. Then follow from step 2 for the dressing.

FISH & SEA FOOD

- Fish and sea food gets cooked very fast. **Overcooking** makes it hard.
- The temperature should be **low moderate** as even a little high temperature makes the sea food tough.
- Sea food is very perishable, so do not buy and keep it for long. Buy fresh and **cook the same day** for good results. Do not use stale seafood.
- When skewering delicate meats like fish and prawns, it is advisable to use **thinner skewers**, then there is less chance of the vegetable or fish to break.

- Always place the tikkas or the seekhs/kebabs **on the grill** or on the wire rack and never directly on a tray. When you place them on a tray, the liquid that drips while grilling keeps collecting around the food and keeps the food wet all the time. This prevents the tandoori food from getting crisp on the outside. Whereas, if the food is placed on the wire rack, the liquid drips down and food remains dry.

Ajwaini Machhi

Ajwain enhances the flavour of the fish.

Serves 4 - 6   *Picture on cover*

½ kg fish - cut into 1½" pieces
3 tbsp dry besan, 1 tbsp lemon juice

1ST MARINADE
juice of 1 lemon, ½ tsp ajwain
½ tsp salt, ½ tsp black pepper

PASTE
1½" piece ginger, 10 flakes garlic
2 onions
1 tbsp mint leaves(poodina), 2 tbsp green coriander(hara dhania)
½ tsp saboot kali mirch (black peppercorns)
3 roasted dry red chillies - roasted on a tawa(gridle)

2ND MARINADE
1 cup yogurt - hang for ½ hour
2 tsp ajwain, ½ tsp jeera, ½ tsp garam masala
¼ tsp kala namak (black salt), ½ tsp red chilli powder, 1½ tsp haldi (turmeric)
1 tsp amchoor, 1 tsp salt, 1½ tbsp oil

BASTING (POURING)
3 tbsp melted butter mixed with ½ tsp ajwain

1. Rub the fish well with besan and lemon juice to remove the fishy odour. Keep aside for 15 minutes. Wash well and pat dry on a kitchen towel. Prick fish all over with a fork or give shallow cuts with a knife.
2. Add all ingredients of the 1st marinade- lemon juice, ajwain, salt and pepper. Keep aside for ½ hour. Drain and wash well.
3. Grind all the ingredients given under paste in a mixer. Keep paste aside.
4. Mix all the ingredients of the 2nd marinade- yogurt, ajwain, jeera, garam masala, kala namak, chilli powder, haldi, amchoor, salt and oil. Add the freshly ground paste also to the marinade.
5. Add fish to the marinade. Coat well with marinade. Keep aside for 1 hour.
6. Heat an electric oven to 160°C or a gas tandoor on gas on low heat.
7. Skewer tikkas on greased skewers or place them on a greased grill (brush grill with oil) and grill for 12 minutes or till coating turns dry and golden brown.
8. Baste (pour) tikkas with ajwani melted butter in between and grill for another 3 minutes. Serve immediately with chilli garlic chutney (see page 119).

Chilli Prawns

Picture on facing page　　　　　*Serves 8-10*

20 medium size prawns
4 tbsp oil
2 tsp cornflour

RED PASTE
5-6 dry, red chillies - soaked in a little water for 15 minutes
2 tbsp chopped onion
1½ tbsp chopped garlic
1 tbsp chopped ginger
15-20 peppercorns (saboot kali mirch)
2 tsp coriander seeds (saboot dhania)
2 tsp cumin (jeera)
2 tsp lemon juice
2 tsp salt, 1½ tbsp vinegar

1. Wash and devein the prawns. Pat dry. Add oil and mix well.
2. For the red paste, soak red chillies in water.
3. Drain the soaked chillies and put them in a grinder. Add all the other ingredients and using the minimum amount of water grind to a paste.
4. Remove the paste to a large bowl. To the paste add cornflour.
5. Add the prawns to the bowl and mix well coating them well. Cover and leave to marinate the prawns in it for 1 hour.
6. Line a baking tray with aluminium foil. Grease the foil.
7. At the time of serving, arrange the marinated prawns on a baking tray lined with foil. Cook in a hot oven at 160°C for 10-12 minutes, basting with oil twice in between.
8. Serve at once, garnished with lemon wedges and fresh coriander.

Note: Be particular about the cooking time of prawns, do not over cook. They tend to get hard if overdone. Also remember to keep them in the oven just 10-15 minutes before serving, as they should be served immediately after they are ready.

Malai Prawns : Recipe on page 79, Chilli Prawns ➤

Machhi Seekh Kebab

Cubes of Sole, marinated twice and spiced with nutmeg.

Serves 6

½ kg of boneless fish, preferably Sole
3 tbsp besan (gram flour), 2 tbsp lemon juice

FOR BOILING FISH
2 flakes garlic, ½ tsp salt

1ST MARINADE
juice of 1 lemon, ½ tsp salt, ½ tsp pepper

2ND MARINADE
1 tbsp ginger - finely grated, 3 green chillies - minced
¼ cup green coriander paste - (grind about 1 cup coriander with 1-2 tbsp water)
½ cup plus 3 tbsp besan- roasted on a griddle (tawa)
½ tsp jaiphal (nutmeg) powder, ¼ tsp haldi, 1½ tsp pepper, ½ tsp salt or to taste
3 tbsp mustard oil or any cooking oil

BASTING (FOR POURING ON THE KEBABS)
1½ tbsp oil or melted butter

1. Rub the fish well with 3 tbsp besan and 2 tbsp lemon juice to remove the fishy odour. Keep aside for 15 minutes. Wash well and pat dry on a kitchen towel.
2. Prick fish all over with a fork or give shallow cuts with a knife.
3. Add all ingredients of 1st marinade. Keep aside for ½ hour. Drain & wash gently.
4. For boiling fish, in a pan put 1 cup water, add garlic, salt and fish. Cook for 10 minutes or till tender. Remove. Cool.
5. Remove all the bones from fish. Grind the de-boned fish in a grinder till smooth.
6. Mix all the ingredients of the 2nd marinade and mix it with the mashed fish. Mix well (Process of mixing is important as all the ingredients have to blend well with the mince). Leave aside for ½ hour in the refrigerator.
7. Heat an oven at 160°C with greased skewers or a gas tandoor at low heat.
8. Take a big ball of the mince mixture and hold a well greased hot skewer carefully in the other hand. Press the mince on to a hot skewer. The mince will immediately stick to the hot skewer. If the skewers are cold the mince will not stick.
9. Make one big seekh on the skewer. Repeat with the left over mince on all the other skewers. Place the skewers in the hot oven or tandoor. Cook for 5-7 minutes, basting with oil in between and changing sides. Cook for another 3 minutes. Gently remove the kebab from the skewers with the help of a cloth.
10. To serve, cut each into 1" pieces and sprinkle chaat masala.

Malai Mahi Tikka

Delicious gilled mahi (fish is also called mahi).Makes an excellent snack.

Serves 4-6

½ kg boneless fish, preferably Sole - cut into 1½" pieces
3 tbsp dry besan (gramflour), 2 tbsp lemon juice

1ST MARINADE
2 tbsp lemon juice, 1 tsp garlic paste
½ tsp salt and ½ tsp pepper

2ND MARINADE
2 egg yolks
1 onion- sliced
¼ cup yogurt - hang in a muslin cloth for 30 minutes
1½ tsp ginger-garlic paste, ½ tsp jeera - roasted and crushed
3 tbsp finely grated processed cheese (Britannia)
4 tbsp cornflour, ½ cup thick cream
¼ tsp red chilli powder, ½ tsp freshly crushed pepper, 1 tsp salt

BASTING (FOR POURING ON THE TIKKAS)
4 tbsp melted butter

1. Rub the fish well with besan and lemon juice to remove the fishy odour. Keep aside for 15 minutes. Wash well and pat dry on a kitchen towel.
2. Prick fish all over with a fork or give shallow cuts with a knife.
3. Add ingredients of 1st marinade to the fish - lemon juice, garlic, salt & pepper. Keep aside ½ hour. Drain, wash gently and pat dry with a kitchen towel.
4. Heat 2 tbsp oil and fry the onions till soft. Cool and grind the onions in a grinder.
5. Mix all ingredients of 2nd marinade, except eggs to onion paste - yoghurt, ginger-garlic paste, jeera, cheese, cornflour, cream, chilli powder, pepper and salt. Make a smooth thick marinade. Put the fish tikkas in this marinade. Keep aside for 2 hours in the refrigerator.
6. Separate egg yolks from egg whites. Beat the egg yolks well and mix them into the marinated fish. Mix well.
7. Heat a gas tandoor on gas at low heat or an electric oven to 160°C. Brush the wire rack or grill of the oven with oil. Place the tikkas pieces on it and grill them for 1 0 minutes overturning them every few minutes. Baste (pour) the tikkas with melted butter every few minutes, and grill till coating turns dry and golden brown. Grill for another 3 minutes.
8. Sprinkle some chaat masala. Serve with poodina chutney (see page 119).

Khatti Meethi Mahi

A whole sweet and sour mahi(fish) cooked in a South Indian style.

Serves 4-6

500 gm whole pomfret
3 tbsp dry besan, 2 tbsp lemon juice
3 tbsp oil

1ST MARINADE
2 tbsp lemon juice, 1 tsp black pepper, ½ tsp salt

OTHER INGREDIENTS
2 tbsp oil, 1 tbsp curry masala (MDH)
a lemon sized ball of tamarind (imli) boiled with ½ cup water and strained to get
3 tbsp tamarind pulp
1 tbsp sugar, 1 tsp salt
2 tsp cornflour, a pinch of tandoori red colour

GRIND TO A PASTE
2 big onions, 1" piece ginger, 3-4 green chillies, 1 tbsp curry leaves

1. Rub the fish well with besan and lemon juice to remove the fishy odour. Keep aside for 15 minutes. Wash well and pat dry on a kitchen towel.
2. Add all ingredients of 1st marinade to the fish. Keep aside for ½ hour.
3. Drain and wash gently. Pat dry & make 3 deep cuts diagonally across each side.
4. Grind onions, ginger, green chillies and curry leaves in a grinder with little water if required. Keep paste aside.
5. In a kadhai heat 2 tbsp oil, add the ground paste and stir fry till light brown.
6. Add curry masala, colour and cornflour, stir for a minute. Add tamarind pulp, sugar and salt. Cook for 5 minutes. Remove, cool & churn in a blender again with little water if required for a smooth thick marinade.
7. Rub marinade on the fish and fill the deep cuts also with this mixture. Keep aside for 3-4 hours. Heat oven to 160°C or a gas tandoor on gas at low heat.
8. Grease skewers well. Skewer the fish from mouth to tail. While skewering a whole fish the skewer should pass along the backbone and parallel to it. (Inserted at the mouth, it should emerge at the tail without puncturing the fish at any other point, this way there is less chance of fish slipping during cooking).
9. Grill the fish for 10 minutes or till the fish turns golden brown. Baste (pour) with melted butter and cook for another 3 minutes, changing sides.
10. Remove and hang the skewer to allow the excess moisture to drip off.
11. Garnish with pepper and serve with til chutney (see page 119).

Methi Mahi Tikka

Cubes of Sole spiced with fenugreek and nutmeg.

Picture on page 2   *Serves*

500 gm boneless Sole fish - cut into 2" cubes
3 tbsp besan and 1 tbsp lemon juice

1ST MARINADE
2 tbsp vinegar or lemon juice
¼ tsp red chilli powder, ½ tsp salt

GRIND TO A FINE PASTE
1 tbsp mint leaves(poodina), 1 tbsp kasoori methi(dry fenugreek leaves)
½ tsp methi daana (fenugreek seeds)
2 tsp ginger-garlic paste

2ND MARINADE
¼ cup thick cream
½ cup yogurt - hang in a muslin cloth for ½ hour
3 tbsp cheese - finely grated (cube)
½ tsp green cardamom (illaichi) - ground
2 tbsp cornflour, 3 cloves (laung) - crushed
2 " stick dalchini(cinnamon), ¼ tsp grated jaiphal (nutmeg)
1 tsp salt, 1 tsp red chilli powder, 1 tbsp oil

BASTING
2 tbsp oil or melted butter mixed with 3 tbsp kasoori methi

1. Rub the fish well with besan and lemon juice to remove the fishy odour. Keep aside for 15 minutes. Wash well and pat dry on a kitchen towel.
2. Prick fish all over with a fork or give shallow cuts with a knife.
3. Marinate with all the ingredients of the 1st marinade. Keep aside ½ hour.
4. Drain, wash gently and pat dry with a kitchen towel.
5. Grind together ginger, garlic, methi daana and mint leaves to a fine paste.
6. Rub the fish tikkas thoroughly with the prepared paste. Keep aside for ½ hour.
7. Mix ingredients of the 2nd marinade in a bowl – cream, yogurt, cheese, kasoori methi, illaichi, cornflour, laung, dalchini, jaiphal, salt, chilli powder and oil.
8. Add tikka pieces to this marinade and coat well. Keep aside for 3-4 hours.
9. Heat an electric oven to 180°C or a gas tandoor on gas at low heat for 15 minutes. Brush the greased wire rack or grill of the oven with oil. Place the tikka pieces on it and grill them for 10-12 minutes overturning and basting with a little melted butter every few minutes till coating turns dry and golden brown.
10. Serve hot with til chutney (see page 119) and sprinkle some chaat masala.

Dhania Fish Tikka

Delicious grilled fish flavoured with coriander.

Picture on page 19   *Serves 4-6*

½ kg boneless fish - cut into 1½" x 1" pieces
3 tbsp dry besan, ½ tsp salt and a pinch of haldi (turmeric powder)

1ST MARINADE
juice of 1 lemon
½ tsp salt, ½ tsp pepper

2ND MARINADE
½ cup thick curd - hang for 30 minutes in muslin cloth
1 tsp cornflour
2 tbsp oil
½ tsp ajwain (carom seeds), 1 tsp salt

GRIND TO A FINE PASTE
½ cup chopped fresh dhania (coriander)
2 tbsp kasoori methi (dry fenugreek leaves)
1 tbsp badam (almonds) - crushed
1 tsp saunf (fennel)
3-4 flakes garlic, ¼" piece ginger, 1 green chilli
1 tbsp lemon juice

BASTING
2 tbsp melted butter mixed with 1 tbsp kasoori methi

1. Rub the fish well with besan and lemon juice to remove the fishy odour. Keep aside for 15 minutes. Wash well and pat dry on a kitchen towel.
2. Prick fish all over with a fork or give shallow cuts with a knife.
3. Add ingredients of 1st marinade-lemon juice, salt & pepper. Keep aside ½ hour.
4. Drain, wash gently and pat dry with a kitchen towel.
5. Grind together dhania, kasoori methi, badam, saunf, ginger, garlic, green chilli and lemon juice to a rough green paste.
6. Mix the green paste with the ingredients of the 2nd marinade- curd, cornflour, oil salt and ajwain. Marinate fish in this paste for at least half an hour.
7. Heat an electric oven to 160°C or a gas tandoor on gas at low heat for 15 minutes.Brush the greased wire rack or grill of the oven with oil. Place the tikka pieces on it and grill them for 10-12 minutes overturning them every few minutes.
8. Baste tikkas with (pour) melted butter mixed with kasoori methi and grill for another 2-3 minutes. Serve hot sprinkled with chaat masala.

Amritsari Khatti Machhi

Fish with a tangy flavour.

Serves 5-6

800 gms fish, preferably boneless Sole - Cut into 2 " pieces (10-12 pieces)
5 tbsp plus 7 tbsp besan, 5 tbsp lemon juice
some chaat masala for sprinkling on top

1ST MARINADE
4 tbsp vinegar or lemon juice
½ tsp red chilli powder, ½ tsp salt

2ND MARINADE
3 tsp ajwain
½ onion- chopped, 5 tsp ginger-garlic paste
2 tsp garam masala
8 tbsp lemon juice
1½ tsp red chilli powder
3 tbsp oil
1½ tsp salt and 1 tsp pepper

BASTING
4 tbsp melted butter

1. Rub the fish well with 5 tbsp besan and lemon juice to remove the fishy odour. Keep aside for 15 minutes. Wash well and pat dry on a kitchen towel.
2. Prick fish all over with a fork or give shallow cuts with a knife.
3. Add ingredients of the 1st marinade to the fish - lemon juice, salt and red chilli powder. Keep aside ½ hour.
4. Drain, wash gently and pat dry with a kitchen towel.
5. Add all ingredients of the 2nd marinade- ajwain, onion, ginger-garlic paste, garam masala, lemon juice, red chilli powder, 3 tbsp oil, pepper and salt. Rub this marinade on the fish & leave the fish to marinate for 2-3 hours in the fridge.
6. At the time of serving, sprinkle 7 tbsp besan on fish and rub it so that the besan lightly coats the fish.
7. Heat an electric oven to 160°C or a gas tandoor on gas at low heat. Brush the greased wire rack or grill of the oven with oil. Place the tikka pieces on it and grill them for 12-15 minutes overturning them every few minutes.
8. Baste (pour) the tikkas with melted butter every few minutes and grill till coating turns dry and golden brown.
9. Sprinkle chaat masala & serve with chilli garlic chutney (see page 119) & onions.

Fish Kebabs

Makes 12

500 gm boneless Sole fish- cut into ½" pieces
3 tbsp besan, 1 tbsp lemon juice

1ST MARINADE
2 tbsp vinegar or lemon juice
¼ tsp pepper
¼ tsp salt

2ND MARINADE
1 tbsp ginger-garlic paste
2 tbsp green coriander - chopped
2 green chillies - chopped
½ tsp garam masala
¼ tsp chilli powder
½ tsp salt or to taste
1 tsp tandoori masala
oil for shallow frying

1. Rub the fish well with besan and lemon juice to remove the fishy odour. Keep aside for 15 minutes. Wash well and pat dry on a kitchen towel.
2. Prick fish all over with a fork or give shallow cuts with a knife.
3. Add ingredients of 1st marinade to the fish - lemon juice, salt and pepper. Keep aside for ½ hour.
4. Drain, wash gently and pat dry with a kitchen towel.
5. Boil 3- 4 cups of water in a pan. Add the fish pieces. Cover the pan and cook the fish for 2-3 minutes or till tender or microwave fish pieces covered in a dish for 5 minutes on power 9. Cool.
6. Remove from fire. Wash fish well. Churn the boiled fish in a mixer till smooth.
7. Add all ingredients of the 2nd marinade- ginger-garlic paste, coriander, green chillies, garam masala, chilli powder, salt and tandoori masala. Mix well.
8. Shape into flat kebabs (flat tikkis). Keep in the fridge for ½ hour.
9. Heat 3 tbsp butter in a shallow pan, and fry the kebabs on low flame till golden brown on both sides.
10. Serve hot sprinkled with chaat masala and with khatti arbi ka salad (see page 120) and khatti meethi chutney (see page 118).

Mahi (fish) Tikka

Serves 6-8

500 gm boneless Singhara or Sole fish - cut into 2" cubes
3 tbsp besan, 1 tbsp lemon juice

1ST MARINADE
2 tbsp vinegar or lemon juice
¼-½ tsp red chilli powder
¼ tsp salt

2ND MARINADE
½ cup curd curd- hang in a muslin cloth for 15 minutes
¼ cup thick cream or malai
2 tsp ginger-garlic paste
½ tsp garam masala powder
½ tsp ajwain (carom seeds)
1 tsp salt
½ tsp pepper

FOR GARNISHING
lemon slices, mint or coriander sprig, some chaat masala

1. Rub the fish well with 3 tbsp besan and 2 tbsp lemon juice to remove the fishy odour. Keep aside for 15 minutes. Wash well and pat dry on a kitchen towel. Prick fish all over with a fork or give shallow cuts with a knife.
2. Marinate with lemon juice, salt and red chilli powder. Keep aside for ½ hour.
3. In a bowl mix all the ingredients of the 2ND marinade- curd, cream, ginger-garlic paste, garam masala, ajwain, salt and pepper.
4. Add tikka pieces and coat well with this marinade. Keep aside for 3-4 hours.
5. Heat an electric oven to 160°C or a gas tandoor on gas at low heat.
6. Skewer tikkas or place them on a well greased wire grill and roast till coating turns dry and golden brown. Baste with a little butter in between. Roast for another 2-3 minutes.
7. Serve hot with dahi poodina chutney (see page 118) and mixed green relish (see page 121). Sprinkle some chat masala.

Note:

- When skewering delicate meats fish, prawns, and vegetables it is advisable to use **thinner skewers**, then there is less chance of the vegetable or fish to break.
- The temperature should be **low moderate** as even a little high temperature makes the sea food tough.

Fish Tandoori

Delicious, succulent fish. Can be served as a snack or with the main meal.

Serves 3-4

500 gms fish - cut into 5-6 pieces, preferably boneless and skinless
3 tbsp besan, 1 tbsp lemon juice
½ tsp salt, ½ tsp red chilli powder

MARINADE
2½ tsp Kashmiri red chilli powder (degi mirch)
½ tsp shah jeera (black cumin), 1 tsp ginger paste, 1 tsp garlic paste
½ tsp tandoori masala
½ tsp garam masala powder
1½ tsp amchoor, 1 tsp dhania powder
2 tbsp lemon juice, ¼ tsp chaat masala
1¼ tsp salt

BASTING
4 tbsp melted butter mixed with ¼ tsp shah jeera (black cumin)

1. Rub the fish well with 3 tbsp besan and 2 tbsp lemon juice to remove the fishy odour. Keep aside for 15 minutes. Wash well and pat dry on a kitchen towel. Prick fish all over with a fork or give shallow cuts with a knife.
2. Mix all ingredients given under marinade. Rub the marinade well all over the fish pieces and let it marinate for 2-3 hours.
3. Heat an electric oven to 160°C or a gas tandoor on gas at low heat. Grease the wire rack and place fish pieces on it. Let it grill for 8-10 minutes.
4. Baste (pour) with melted butter mixed with shah jeera. Grill again for 8-10 minutes till well cooked and crisp. The time of grilling will depend on the thickness of the fish and may vary a little.
5. Sprinkle chaat masala and serve hot with dahi poodina chutney (see page 118) and sirke waale pyaaz (see page 120) or garnished papad (see page 126).

Note:

- A small fish (pomfret) can be made whole in this way.
- While grilling, always place fish pieces (or a whole fish) on a rack with the drip tray below it as it will leave some liquid which will drip down. If the fish is placed on a tray/thali the water will remain around the fish and hence make it soggy and it will not get crisp.

Tandoori Makai Mirch : Recipe on page 85 ➢
Subz Kakori : Recipe on page 94 ➢

Tandoori Masala Pomfret

A whole fish! Your selection of pomfret is very important for a mouth-watering sight & taste.

Picture on page 1   *Serves 2-3*

500 gm whole pomfret
3 tbsp besan, juice of 1 lemon

1ST MARINADE
juice of 1 lemon, ½ tsp salt, ¼ tsp red chilli powder

2ND MARINADE
1 cup yogurt - hang for 1 hour in a muslin cloth, 2 tbsp besan
2 tsp garam masala, 2 tsp red chilli powder, 1 tsp salt
2 tbsp oil, a pinch of tandoori red colour

GRIND TO A PASTE
2" piece ginger, 8-10 flakes garlic
1 onion, 1 tsp black peppercorns, 1 tsp roasted jeera (bhuna jeera)
1 tbsp green coriander

BASTING (POURING ON THE FISH)
3 tbsp melted butter

1. Rub the fish well with 3 tbsp besan and lemon juice to remove the fishy odour. Keep aside for 15 minutes. Wash well and pat dry on a kitchen towel.
2. Marinate fish with all ingredients of the 1st marinade. Keep aside for ½ hour.
3. Drain and wash gently. Pat dry & make 3 deep cuts diagonally across each side.
4. Grind ginger, garlic, onion, peppercorns, jeera & coriander to a paste in a grinder.
5. Mix all the ingredients of the 2nd marinade - yogurt, besan, garam masala, red chilli powder, salt, oil, colour and the ground paste. Keep paste aside.
6. Fill the deep cuts of the fish with the marinade. Rub the left over marinade on the fish. Keep aside for 2-3 hours.
7. Heat an electric oven to 160°C or a gas tandoor on gas on low heat.
8. Brush the skewer well with oil. Skewer the fish from mouth to tail. While skewering a whole fish the skewer should pass along the backbone and parallel to it. (Inserted at the mouth, it should emerge at the tail without puncturing the fish at any other point). This way there is less chance of fish slipping during cooking.
9. Grill the fish for 10 minutes or till the fish turns golden brown. Baste (pour) with melted butter and cook for another 3 minutes, changing sides.
10. Remove gently and hang the skewer to allow the excess moisture to drip off.
11. Serve with dahi poodina chutney (see page 118).

Malai Prawns

Serves 6-8   *Picture on page 67*

20 large prawns
3 tbsp butter melted and mixed with 1 tsp white pepper - for basting

1ST MARINADE
2-3 tbsp lemon juice
1 tsp salt, ½ tsp red chilli powder
2 tbsp oil

2ND MARINADE
1 cup thick curd - hang for 15 minutes
4 tbsp thick cream
2-4 tbsp grated cheese, preferably mozzarella
1 egg
2 tbsp oil
¾ tsp salt
1 tbsp cornflour
1 tbsp ginger paste
2 tbsp chopped coriander

1. Devein and wash prawns. Pat dry them on a clean kitchen towel.
2. Marinate the prawns with the first marinade – salt, red chilli, lemon juice and oil for ½ hour.
3. For the 2nd marinade, mix cream, cheese, egg, oil, cornflour, ginger paste, salt and coriander with the hung curd.
4. Pick up the prawns discarding the lemon juice. Marinate them in the curd mixture for 2-3 hours or even more, but refrigerate while being marinated.
5. Arrange the marinated prawns on a greased wire rack or baking tray. Bake in a hot oven at 160°C for 10 minutes.
6. Melt some butter and mix some white pepper in it. Turn the prawns once in between during baking and baste with this melted butter to flavour them. Cook till tender.
7. Serve with mint chutney mixed with a little hung curd. Garnish with onion rings.

Note: Be particular about the baking time of prawns, do not over bake. They tend to get hard if overbaked. Also remember to keep them in the oven just 10-15 minutes before serving.

Always grease the wire rack, skewers or grill nicely with oil to avoid the kebabs sticking to the grill.

Tandoori Jhinga

Serves 6-8

20 large prawns
3 tbsp butter melted and mixed with 1 tsp white pepper - for basting

1ST MARINADE
2-3 tbsp lemon juice
1 tsp salt, ½ tsp red chilli powder
2 tbsp oil

2ND MARINADE
1 cup thick curd - hang for 15 minutes
4 tbsp thick cream
2-4 tbsp grated cheese, preferably mozzarella
1 egg white
2 tbsp oil
¾ tsp salt, ½ tsp red chilli powder, 2 tsp tandoori masala
1 tbsp cornflour, ¼ tsp garam masala
1 tbsp ginger paste, a pinch of tandoori colour
2 tbsp chopped coriander

GRIND TO A PASTE IN A SPICE GRINDER
1 small onion, 1 tbsp ginger paste
1½ tbsp chopped coriander, 1 tsp mint leaves (poodina)

1. Devein and wash prawns. Pat dry them on a clean kitchen towel.
2. Marinate prawns with the 1st marinade – salt, red chilli powder, lemon juice and oil for ½ hour.
3. Grind onion, coriander, ginger and mint leaves in grinder. Keep the paste aside.
4. Mix hung curd, cream, cheese, egg white, oil, salt, red chilli powder, tandoori masala, cornflour, garam masala, ginger paste, colour, chopped coriander and the ground paste to the hung curd.
5. Pick up the prawns discarding the lemon juice. Marinate them in the curd mixture for 2-3 hours or even more, but refrigerate while being marinated.
6. Arrange the marinated prawns on a greased wire rack or baking tray. Bake in a hot oven at 160°C for 10 minutes.
7. Melt some butter and mix some white pepper in it. Turn the prawns once in between during baking and baste with this melted butter to flavour them. Cook till tender.
8. Serve with poodina chutney (see page 119) & garnished papad (see page 126).

Note: Be particular about the oven time, do not over grill the prawns.

VEGETARIAN

- Cut the pieces of food according to the space in between the wires of the grill. If the distance between the wires of the rack is too wide, and there is a chance of your piece slipping, then cover the wire rack with a well greased aluminium foil.
- The size of the tikkas should not be too small, because after getting cooked they shrink. A very small piece after getting cooked can turn hard after some time.
- While skewering or placing pieces of vegetables, the pieces should be arranged such that there is atleast 1" gap between them so that each piece can get it's own space and heat all around to get cooked properly.

- When skewering vegetables, it is advisable to use thinner skewers, then there is less chance of the vegetable or fish to break.
- Pastes like raw papaya paste, ginger-garlic paste, onion paste, coriander paste or chilli paste should be made with as little water as possible.
- To keep the tandoori food soft and succulent, baste food with some melted butter/ oil or sometimes with the left over marinade. To baste, just pour the oil/melted butter on the food that is being barbecued when it is a little more than half done.

Achaari Paneer Tikka

Pickle flavoured masala paneer tikka.

Picture on page 127   *Makes 10-12*

400 gms paneer - cut into 1½" rectangles of ¾-1" thickness
2 tsp ginger-garlic paste
1 tsp cornflour
1 cup curd - hang in a muslin cloth for ½ hour
2 tbsp oil
½ tsp haldi (turmeric) powder
1 tsp amchoor (dried mango powder)
1 tsp dhania powder, ½ tsp garam masala
1 tsp salt or to taste, ½ tsp sugar
1 onion - chopped finely
2 green chillies - chopped
some chaat masala to sprinkle
some melted butter/oil for basting the tikkas

ACHAARI MASALA
1 tbsp saunf (aniseeds)
½ tsp sarson (mustard seeds)
a pinch of methi daana (fenugreek seeds)
½ tsp kalonji (onion seeds)
½ tsp jeera (cumin seeds)

1. Collect seeds of achaari masala- saunf, rai, methi daana, kalonji and jeera together.
2. Heat 2 tbsp oil. Add the collected seeds together to the hot oil. Let saunf change colour.
3. Add onions and chopped green chillies. Cook till onions turn golden brown.
4. Reduce heat. Add haldi, amchoor, dhania powder, garam masala, salt and sugar. Mix. Remove from fire. Let it cool down.
5. Beat curd till smooth. Add garlic-ginger paste and cornflour. Add the onion masala also to the curd.
6. Add the paneer cubes to the curd. Marinate till serving time.
7. At serving time, rub oil generously over the grill of the oven or wire rack of a gas tandoor. Place paneer on the greased wire rack or grill of the oven.
8. Heat an oven to 180°C or a gas tandoor on moderate flame. Grill paneer for 15 minutes. Spoon some oil or melted butter on the paneer pieces in the oven or tandoor and grill further for 5 minutes. Serve hot sprinkled with chaat masala.

Malai Khumb

Serves 6-8   *Picture on page 1*

200 gm mushrooms - choose big ones
juice of ½ lemon
1 tbsp butter - melted, for basting (pouring on the tikkas)
chaat masala to sprinkle

MARINADE
4 tbsp thick cream
1 cup thick curd - hang in a muslin cloth for 15 minutes
2-4 tbsp grated cheese, preferably mozzarella
2 tbsp oil
1 tbsp cornflour
1 tbsp ginger paste
¾ tsp salt
2 tbsp chopped coriander

1. Wash mushrooms well. Trim the stalks neatly.
2. Boil 4-5 cups water with 1 tsp salt and juice of ½ lemon. As soon as the boil comes, add the mushrooms. Let them boil for a minute. Strain and pat dry them on a clean kitchen towel.
3. Squeeze curd and transfer to a bowl. Mix cream, cheese, oil, cornflour, ginger paste, salt and coriander to the hung curd.
4. Marinate the mushrooms in the curd mixture till serving time.
5. To serve, preheat the oven to 180°C. Arrange the marinated mushrooms on a greased wire rack with head side up. Pat the left over marinade on the mushroom heads. You can arrange these on thin skewers also. Grill in a hot oven at 180°C for 15-20 minutes till the coating turns dry.
6. Melt some butter. In between, pour some melted butter on the mushrooms.
7. Remove from oven when done. Sprinkle chaat masala. Serve with mint chutney mixed with a little hung curd. Garnish with onion rings.

Note:
- While threading mushrooms, use thin skewers. Push the skewers gently. They should be woven through the vegetable. This way there are less chances of the food slipping down.
- While skewering or placing pieces of chicken, mutton, fish or any vegetable, the pieces should be such arranged that there is atleast 1" gap between them so that each piece can get it's own space to get cooked.

Bhutte Ke Seekh

Corn is very popular in India. Here corn makes a crunchy kebab.

Picture on page 107   *Makes 7-8 pieces*

4 tender, large fresh bhuttas - grated (1 cup) or 1 cup tinned or frozen corn - blend
½ of the tinned or frozen corn in a mixer and keep ½ whole kernels
2 potatoes - boiled & grated
1 onion - chopped
2 green chillies - chopped finely
2 tbsp chopped fresh coriander
½ tbsp chopped mint (poodina)
½ tsp garam masala powder
1 tbsp melted butter
½ tsp pepper powder
1 tsp salt or to taste
3 tbsp besan (gramflour) - roasted on a tawa for 1 minute till fragrant
juice of 1 lemon
3 tbsp melted butter for basting (pouring on the kebabs)

1. Mash the boiled potatoes and the corn. Mix well.
2. Add onions, green chillies, coriander, mint, garam masala, 1 tbsp melted butter, salt and pepper. Check seasoning.
3. Add roasted besan and lemon juice.
4. Oil and wipe the skewers. Heat an oven to 180°C or a gas tandoor on moderate flame for 15 minutes.
5. Press mixture into sausage-shaped kebabs on the skewers, making a long kebab of the corn paste over the skewer. Cook for about 5 minutes in a hot tandoor or grill. Pour some melted butter on the kebabs to baste them when they get half done. Turn side and grill for 8-10 minutes or till golden brown.
6. Serve with khatti meethi chutney (see page 118) and mixed green relish (see page 121).

Note: If you wish you could even shallow fry the kebabs in a pan on medium heat in 3 tbsp oil.

Tandoori Makai Mirch

Paneer cubes are mixed with mozzarella cheese to hold the diced paneer and corn together, because on cooking the cheese melts, binding the two together.

Serves 4   *Picture on page 77*

4 medium size capsicums

MARINADE
2 tbsp lemon juice, 1 tsp ginger paste, ½ tsp garlic paste, 1 tbsp oil, ¾ tsp salt

STUFFING
100 gm paneer - finely cut into ¼" cubes (1 cup)
½ cup grated mozzarella cheese
½ cup corn kernels - tinned or freshly boiled
1 tbsp chopped cashews and 8-10 kishmish
¼ tsp hing (asafoetida), 1 tsp jeera (cumin seeds) and ½ tsp sarson (mustard seeds)
1 small onion - cut into half and then into rings, to get shredded onion
1 tbsp green coriander - chopped, 2 tbsp oil
½ tsp red chilli powder, ¾ tsp salt, ½ tsp garam masala, ¼ tsp amchoor

BASTING
2 tbsp oil or melted butter

1. Cut a slice from the top of each capsicum. Scoop out the center with the help of a knife. Mix all the ingredients of the marinade and rub liberally on the inside of the capsicums. Cover with caps and leave aside for ½ hour.
2. Take a heavy bottom kadhai and heat oil. Put in the hing, jeera, and sarson. Wait till jeera turns golden.
3. Add onions and cook till soft. Add cashews and kishmish. Stir. Add red chilli powder, salt, garam masala and amchoor.
4. Add corn and cook for 1 minute. Add paneer and mix well. Remove from fire. Add mozzarella cheese. Mix. Keep filling aside.
5. Stuff the capsicums with this filling. They should be stuffed well but not to bursting point. Rub oil on the stuffed capsicums. Cover with the caps and secure them with wooden toothpicks.
6. Oil and wipe the skewers. Skewer the capsicums. Small onions or pieces of potatoes can be used in-between to prevent them from slipping. Put the skewers into the oven or the gas tandoor and cook for 10 minutes or till they turn blackish at some places. Turn 1-2 times in-between to grill evenly. Serve.

Note: Stuffed capsicums can be placed on the wire-rack or grill rubbed with some oil, if you do not have skewers. It is not necessary to fasten them with tooth picks.

Tandoori Paneer ki Subzi

A delightful paneer dish which is relished with meals as a side dish.

Picture on facing page   *Serves 4*

250 gms paneer - cut into 1" cubes
¾ tsp salt
¼ tsp red chilli powder
1 tsp lemon juice
1 tbsp oil
2 capsicums - cut into fine rings
2 onions - cut into fine rings
¼ tsp kaala namak (black salt), ¼ tsp salt
2 tsp tandoori masala
¼ tsp haldi (turmeric powder) or a pinch of tandoori red colour

GRIND TO A ROUGH PASTE WITHOUT ANY WATER
1½" piece ginger, 2-3 green chillies
1 tsp jeera (cumin seeds)
3-4 flakes garlic - optional

BASTING (POURING ON THE PANEER)
1 tbsp oil or melted butter

1. Grind garlic, ginger, jeera and green chillies to a thick rough paste. Do not add water. Keep the ginger paste aside.
2. Add salt, chilli powder and lemon juice to the paste. Add a little haldi or colour to the paste.
3. Cut paneer into 1" squares. Apply ¾ of this paste nicely on all the pieces. Keep the left over paste aside.
4. Grill this paneer on a greased wire rack and grill at 180C for 10 minutes. Baste (pour) with melted butter or oil and grill for another 5 minutes till it is dry and slightly crisp on the outside. Keep aside till serving time.
5. At serving time, heat 1 tbsp oil in a kadhai. Fry onion and capsicum rings for a few minutes till onions turn transparent. Keep aside a few capsicum rings for garnishing.
6. Add the ginger paste and few drops of lemon juice. Add kala namak and salt.
7. Add tandoori paneer pieces. Sprinkle tandoori masala. Toss for a minutes till the paneer turns soft and is heated properly.
8. Serve immediately, garnished with the capsicum rings kept aside and garnished papad (see page 126).

Banjaara tandoori Tangri : Recipe on page 21, Tandoori Paneer Ki Subzi ➢

Baby Corn Bullets

Enjoy it rolled up in roomali rotis with some onion slices mixed with hari chutney!

Serves 4-5

200 gm baby corns - keep whole
juice of ½ lemon
1-2 capsicums - cut into 1" pieces
8 cherry tomatoes or 1 large tomato - cut into 8 pieces & pulp removed
1 onion - cut into fours & separated or 4 spring onions (keep white part whole)
1- 2 tbsp melted butter for basting
some chaat masala - to sprinkle

MARINADE
1½ cups thick curd - hang for 30 minutes
2 tsp cornflour
2 tbsp thick cream or malai
¼ tsp ajwain (carom seeds)
1 tbsp thick ginger-garlic paste (squeeze out the liquid)
½ tsp kala namak (black salt)
¼ tsp haldi
1 tbsp tandoori masala
¼ tsp red chilli powder
¾ tsp salt

1. Boil 4-5 cups water with 2 tsp salt, ¼ tsp haldi and juice of ½ lemon. Add baby corns to boiling water. After the boil returns, boil for 1 minute or till slightly soft. Strain and wipe dry the corns on a clean kitchen towel. Keep aside.
2. Mix all ingredients of the marinade in a large bowl.
3. Rub oil generously on a wire rack or grill of the oven.
4. Add baby corns first to the marinade in the bowl and mix well to coat the marinade. Remove from bowl and arrange on the greased rack. In the remaining marinade in the bowl, add onion, capsicum and tomatoes. Leave these in the bowl itself. Marinate all for atleast ½ hour.
5. Grill baby corns first in an oven at 200°C for 15 minutes or roast in a gas tandoor. Pour a little melted butter on them. Put the onion and capsicum also along with the corns and grill for another 10 minutes. Lastly put the tomatoes in the oven with the onion-capsicum and grill further for 2-3 minutes.
6. Serve sprinkled with some chat masala, alongwith lemon wedges.

Kebab Hara Bhara

Serves 8

1 cup channe ki dal (split gram)
1 bundle (600 gm) spinach - only leaves, chopped very finely
3 tbsp oil
3 slices bread - broken into pieces and churned in a mixer to get fresh crumbs
3 tbsp cornflour
2 green chillies - chopped finely
½ tsp red chilli powder, ½ tsp garam masala, ¾ tsp salt or to taste
½ tsp amchoor (dried mango powder)
½ cup grated paneer (75 gm)
¼ cup chopped green coriander

CRUSH TOGETHER
½ tsp jeera, seeds of 2 moti illaichi
3-4 saboot kali mirch, 2-3 laung

1. Crush jeera, seeds of moti illaichi, kali mirch and laung together.
2. Clean, wash dal. Pressure cook dal with the above crushed spices, ½ tsp salt and 2 cups water. After the first whistle, keep the cooker on slow fire for 15 minutes. Remove from fire and keep aside.
3. After the pressure drops down, mash the hot dal with a karchhi or a potato masher. If there is any water, mash the dal on fire and dry the dal as well while you are mashing it. Remove from fire.
4. Discard stem of spinach and chop leaves very finely. Wash in several changes of water. Leave the chopped spinach in the strainer for 15 minutes so that the water drains out.
5. Heat 3 tbsp oil in a kadhai. Squeeze and add spinach. Stir for 8-10 minutes till spinach is absolutely dry and well fried.
6. Add paneer and coriander. Cook for 1 minute. Remove from fire and keep aside.
7. Mix dal with - fresh bread crumbs, cornflour, spinach-paneer, green chillies, salt and masalas. Make small balls. Flatten slightly.
8. Cook them on a tawa with just 2-3 tbsp oil till brown on both sides. When done shift them on the sides of the tawa so that they turn crisp and the oil drains out while more kebabs can be added to the hot oil in the centre of the tawa. Remove the kebabs on paper napkins.
9. Serve hot with hari chutney.

Note: If the kebabs break on frying, roll them in dry maida before frying.

Reshmi Paneer Tikka

Extremely soft tikkas cooked finally in cream.

Serves 4-5

250 gms paneer - cut into 1½" cubes (8 pieces)
3 tbsp besan (gram flour)
2 tbsp curd
1 tsp salt
¼ tsp red chilli powder
½ tsp garam masala
a few drops orange red colour
1 tbsp lemon juice
2 capsicums - cut into 1" pieces
2 onions - cut into 1" pieces
2 tbsp oil

GRIND TOGETHER TO A PASTE
1½" piece ginger, 3-4 flakes garlic
1 tsp jeera (cumin seeds)
seeds of 2 chhoti illaichi
2-3 green chillies
2 tbsp chopped coriander

FINAL INGREDIENTS
4-5 tbsp thick cream or fresh malai - beaten well till smooth
3-4 tbsp chopped poodina (mint) leaves
1 tsp lemon juice, chaat masala

1. Grind ginger, garlic, jeera, chhoti illaichi, coriander and green chillies to a paste.
2. Add besan, curd, salt, chilli powder, garam masala and lemon juice to the paste. Add enough orange colour to the paste to get a nice colour.
3. Cut paneer into 1½" cubes. Put the paste in a big bowl and add the paneer pieces and mix well so as to coat the paste nicely on all the pieces. Add the onion and capsicum pieces also and mix lightly. Keep aside till serving time.
4. Heat an oven to 180°C or a gas tandoor on moderate flame. Grill the paneer pieces and vegetables by passing through skewers and keeping in a hot oven on a greased wire rack. Keep in the oven for 10-12 minutes. Remove from oven.
5. Heat malai or cream in a clean kadhai on very low flame, to make it just warm. Do not let it turn into ghee by keeping on the fire for a longer time.
6. Add the grilled paneer and vegetable pieces. Toss gently and remove from fire.
7. Serve with garnished papad (see page 126) sprinkled with chopped poodina, chaat masala and lemon juice.

Poodina Kaju Kebabs

Cashew kebabs stuffed with a minty filling.

Serves 6-8

15 cashewnuts - ground to a coarse powder in a small spice grinder
4 slices of bread - broken into pieces and ground in a mixer to get fresh crumbs
2 big potatoes - chopped
2 small onions - chopped
¾ cup shelled peas
½ of a small cauliflower - cut into small florets
1" piece ginger - crushed to a paste
5-6 flakes garlic - crushed to a paste
½ tsp red chilli powder
½ tsp garam masala
1½ tsp salt or to taste
2 tsp tomato sauce
1 green chilli - finely chopped
2 tbsp chopped fresh coriander
4 tbsp cornflour

FILLING
2-3 tbsp very finely chopped poodina
½ small onion - chopped finely
¼ tsp amchoor
¼ tsp salt

1. Pressure cook potatoes, cauliflower, onion and peas with 1 cup water to give 2 whistles. Keep on low flame for 5 minutes. Remove from fire. Cool. Drain and leave in a sieve for about 5 minutes to remove excess moisture.
2. Mash the vegetables and add ginger, garlic, red chilli powder, garam masala, salt and tomato sauce.
3. Add green chilli, fresh coriander, cornflour, cashewnuts and fresh bread crumbs.
4. Mix all ingredients of the filling together. Keep aside.
5. Break off small balls of the vegetable mixture and pat them into flat circular shapes about ½" thick, with wet hands.
6. Stuff a little of the filling and form a ball. Shape again into a flat disc.
7. Heat 4-5 tbsp oil in a frying pan or on a tawa and fry gently over medium heat, turning once.
8. Remove on a kitchen towel to remove excess oil.
9. Serve hot with poodina chutney.

Exotic Veg Platter
and Barbecue Sauce

Serves 8

250 gm paneer - cut into large (1½") cubes
200 gm (10) large mushrooms - trim ends of the stalks, leaving them whole
100 gm babycorns - blanched with a pinch of haldi and 1 tsp salt in 3 cups water
2 capsicums - cut into large cubes
8 cherry tomatoes or 1 large tomato - cut into 8 pieces & pulp removed
1 large onion - cut into fours & separated

MARINADE
1 cup thick curd - hang for 30 minutes in a muslin cloth
2 tbsp thick cream
2 tbsp oil
1 tbsp cornflour
1 tbsp thick ginger-garlic paste
½ tsp black salt
¼ tsp haldi or tandoori colour
2 tsp tandoori masala
½ tsp red chilli powder
¾ tsp salt or to taste

BARBECUE SAUCE
3 tbsp butter or oil
4-5 flakes garlic - crushed
2 large tomatoes - pureed till smooth
¼ cup ready made tomato puree
¼ tsp red chilli powder
½ tsp pepper
¾ tsp salt or to taste
¼ tsp sugar
½ tsp worcestershire sauce
½ tsp soya sauce

1. Rub oil generously on a wire rack or grill of the oven.
2. Mix all ingredients of the marinade.
3. Add paneer, mushrooms and babycorns to the marinade and mix well to coat the marinade.
4. Remove from bowl and arrange on the greased wire rack or on greased wooden

skewers. In the remaining marinade which is sticking to the sides of the bowl, add onion, capsicum and tomatoes. Leave these in the bowl itself. Marinate all for atleast ½ hour.

5. Grill paneer and vegetables in the oven at 180°C/410°F for 12-15 minutes or roast in a gas tandoor, spooning a little oil (basting) on them in between.

6. For the barbecue sauce - heat oil or butter in a kadhai. Add garlic and cook till light brown. Add tomatoes, tomato puree and red chilli powder and cook for 5 minutes till well blended. Add all other ingredients and ½ cup water to get a thin sauce. Boil. Simmer for 2 minutes. Remove from fire and keep aside.

7. At serving time, heat 2 tbsp oil in a large non stick pan or a big kadhai and add the onion and capsicum. Toss for 1-2 minutes. Reduce flame.

8. Add grilled paneer, mushroom and babycorns. Keep them spread out in the pan on fire for 3-4 minutes on low heat, stirring occasionally. Add the tomatoes.

9. To serve, put some hot sauce on the serving plate. Arrange grilled vegetables on the sauce with or without skewers. Pour some hot sauce over the vegetables. Serve at once. You may serve the vegetables on rice too and serve the extra sauce in a separate sauce boat.

Note:

- When skewering delicate vegetables it is advisable to use thinner skewers, then there is less chance of the vegetable to break.
- To keep the tandoori food soft and succulent, it is important to baste the food with a little melted butter/oil or sometimes the left over marinade. To baste, just pour the oil/butter on the food that is being barbecued when it is a little more than half done.

Subz Kakori

Very soft and delicious vegetarian seekh kebabs.

Picture on page 77   *Serves 4-5*

3 potatoes (medium) - boiled
(250 gm) 2 cups jimikand (yam) - chopped and boiled
½ cup crumbled paneer
4 tbsp cashewnuts - ground
1 tsp ginger paste
1 tsp garlic paste
1 big onion - very finely chopped (1 cup)
2 green chillies - very finely chopped
2 tbsp green coriander - very finely chopped
1 tsp bhuna jeera (cumin roasted)
1 tsp red chilli powder, ¼ tsp amchoor
2 bread slices - crumbled in a grinder to get fresh crumbs
1½ tsp salt, or to taste
a pinch of tandoori red colour

BASTING
2 tbsp melted butter or oil

GARNISH
tandoori khatta masala or chaat masala

1. Boil the potatoes. Peel and mash.
2. Pressure cook chopped yam with ½ cup water and ½ tsp salt to give 3 whistles. Remove from fire. After the pressure drops, keep it on fire to dry, if there is any excess water. Mash it to a paste.
3. Mix mashed potatoes, yam and all other ingredients, making a slightly stiff dough.
4. Oil and wipe the skewers. Heat the gas tandoor or oven. Remove the wire rack. Press into sausage-shaped kebabs on the skewers and cook for about 5 minutes in a hot oven at 180°C or a gas tandoor. Pour some melted butter on the kebabs to baste them when they get half done. Turn side and grill for 5-7 minutes or till golden brown. If you do not wish to grill the kebabs, shallow fry in 2 tbsp oil in a pan on low heat, turning sides till browned evenly.
5. Sprinkle some tandoori or chaat masala and serve with onion rings and lemon wedges.

Note: Turn kebabs on the skewers only after they are half done, otherwise they tend to break.

Hare Chholia Ke Kebab

There are unlimited combinations for making vegetable kebabs, here fresh green gram has been used to churn out deliciously succulent kebabs.

Makes 14   Picture on page 97

2 cups fresh green gram (hara chholia)
½ cup besan (gramflour) - roasted on a tawa for 1 minute, or till fragrant
2 slices bread - broken into pieces and churned in a mixer to get fresh crumbs
1 cup yogurt- hang in a muslin cloth for 30 minutes
1 small onion - chopped
1 tbsp ginger-garlic paste
3-4 green chillies - chopped
10 -12 fresh curry leaves
1 tbsp tandoori masala
1 tsp salt or to taste
1 tsp jeera
3 tbsp oil plus oil for shallow frying
2-3 tbsp maida (plain flour)

CRUSH TOGETHER
1 tbsp saboot dhania (coriander seeds), 1 tsp roasted jeera (bhuna jeera)
½ tsp saboot kali mirch (black peppercorns)

1. Crush saboot dhania, bhuna jeera and saboot kali mirch on a chakla-belan (rolling board-pin).
2. Clean, wash hara chholia. Pressure cook hara chhole with the above crushed spices, ½ tsp salt and 1 cup water. Give one whistle. Remove from fire and keep aside. After the pressure drops down, mash the hot hara chholia with a potato masher or a karchhi. If there is any water, mash and dry the chholia on fire. Remove from fire.
3. Heat 3 tbsp oil, add jeera, let it change colour. Add chopped onion, ginger-garlic paste, chopped green chillies and curry leaves. Cook till onions turn light brown.
4. Add mashed chholia, pepper, salt, roasted besan, tandoori masala and hung yogurt. Cook for 5 minutes or till dry. Remove from fire. Cool.
5. Add bread crumbs and mix well.
6. Make marble sized balls of the chholia mixture. Flatten to form a kebab of about 2" diameter.
7. Roll in maida and shallow fry 3-4 pieces at a time on a hot tawa in 6 tbsp oil. Turn sides till both sides are crisp. Remove the kebabs on paper napkins. Serve.

Hari Seekh Salaad

An unusual, roasted green salad on skewers. Good to start the meal!

Picture on facing page   *Serves 6*

12 big spinach leaves
1 medium broccoli - broken into small florets
5 whole, white part of spring onions, choose big ones
12 cabbage leaves - separated

MARINADE
1¼ cups yoghurt - hang for ½ hour in a muslin cloth
1 onion - grind to a paste, 1 tbsp freshly ground pepper
1 tsp garam masala, ½ tsp amchoor
1½ tbsp oil, 1¼ tsp salt

BASTING
left over marinade

1. Clean and wash all the vegetables. Pat dry the spinach and cabbage leaves on a clean kitchen towel.
2. Boil 4 cups water with 1 tsp salt and 1 tsp sugar. Add broccoli. Let it come to a boil. Boil for 1 minute. Remove from fire. Let it be in hot water for 5 minutes. Drain and refresh in cold water. Wipe dry on a clean kitchen towel.
3. Mix all the ingredients of the marinade – yoghurt, onion paste, pepper, garam masala, amchoor, and 1½ tbsp oil.
4. Take one vegetable at a time and spread the marinade on each vegetable or leaf on both the sides thoroughly. Mix well, leave aside for 1 hour mixing atleast twice in between.
5. Oil and wipe the skewers. Heat the oven at 180°C or gas tandoor on moderate heat.
6. Skewer the vegetables - thread them starting with broccoli, then fold a cabbage leaf and insert, fold a spinach leaf once and then fold again (like a pan) and insert, then insert a whole spring onion and then again another folded cabbage leaf and spinach leaf in the same skewer, repeating till the skewer gets fully covered (cabbage and spinach leaf have been threaded twice).
7. Spread the left over marinade on the skewered vegetables with hand.
8. Put the skewers in the oven or tandoor and cook for 2 minutes.
9. Take out the skewer carefully and baste them again with the marinade. Put them back into the tandoor or oven. Cook for 5 minutes. Serve hot.

Hara Chholia Ke Kebab : Recipe on page 95, Hari Seekh Salaad ➢

Tandoori Bharwaan Aloo

Serves 6

3 big (longish) potatoes
some chaat masala to sprinkle

FILLING
3 almonds - crushed with a belan (rolling pin), 4 tbsp grated paneer (50 gm)
1 tbsp poodina (mint) leaves - chopped, 1 green chilli - deseeded and chopped
¼ tsp garam masala, ¼ tsp red chilli powder, ¼ tsp salt, a pinch amchoor

COVERING
½ cup thick curd - hang in a muslin cloth for 30 minutes
1 tbsp ginger paste
¼ tsp red chilli powder, ¾ tsp salt, ¼ tsp orange tandoori colour or haldi

CRUSH TOGETHER TO A ROUGH POWDER
1 tsp shah jeera (black cumin), seeds of 2 moti illaichi (brown cardamom)
2-3 blades of javitri (mace), 6-8 saboot kali mirch (peppercorns)

1. Boil potatoes in salted water till just tender. When they are no longer hot, peel skin.
2. Mix crushed almonds with mint leaves, green chillies, 4 tbsp grated paneer, ¼ tsp salt, ¼ tsp garam masala, ¼ tsp red chilli and a pinch of amchoor.
3. Grind or crush shah jeera, seeds of moti illaichi, peppercorns, and 2-3 pinches of javitri to a coarse powder.
4. To the paneer mixture, add ¼-½ teaspoon of the above freshly ground spice powder also. Keep the leftover powder aside.
5. Mix hung curd, ginger paste, the left over freshly ground powder and red chilli powder and salt. Add haldi or orange colour.
6. Run the tip of a fork on the surface of the potatoes, making the surface rough. (The rough surface holds the masalas well).
7. Cut each potato into 2 halves, vertically. Scoop out, just a little, to get a small cavity in each potato with the back of a teaspoon. Stuff with paneer filling.
8. With a spoon apply the curd mixture on the outside (backside) of the potatoes and on the rim also (not on the filling).
9. Grill potatoes in a gas tandoor or a preheated oven at 210°C/410°F for 15 minutes on a greased wire rack till they get slightly dry.
10. Spoon some oil or melted butter on them (baste) and then grill further for 10 minutes till the coating turns absolutely dry. Sprinkle some chaat masala and serve hot.

Dal Poodina Kebab

Delicious and quick to prepare.

Serves 10-12

1½ cups chane ki dal
1 tsp salt
½" piece ginger
4-5 flakes garlic
2½ cups water
4 slices bread - broken into pieces and churned in a mixer to get fresh crumbs
½ tsp garam masala
½ tsp amchoor (dried mango powder)
2-3 tbsp maida (plain flour) - to coat

FILLING
2-3 tbsp very finely chopped poodina
1 small onion - chopped finely
1 green chilli - chopped finely
¼ tsp amchoor
¼ tsp salt

1. Clean, wash dal. Pressure cook dal, salt, ginger, garlic and 2½ cups water together. After the first whistle, keep the cooker on low flame for 15 minutes.
2. After the pressure drops down, mash the dal while it is hot, with a karchhi. Keep aside.
3. Add fresh bread crumbs, amchoor and garam masala to the boiled and mashed dal. Add salt to taste. Keep aside.
4. Mix all ingredients of the filling in a small bowl.
5. Make marble sized balls of the dal paste. Flatten them. Put ½ tsp of poodina mixture. Form a ball again. Flatten to form a kebab.
6. Roll in maida and deep fry 3-4 pieces at a time.
7. Dot each kebab with dahi poodina chutney with a spoon. Serve with garnished papad (see page 126). Sprinkle chaat masala.

Note: If the kebabs break on frying, add 1-2 tbsp of maida or an egg white to the mixture.

Haryali Paneer Tikka

Paneer tikka coated with a green coloured chutney.

Picture on page 117   *Serves 6*

400 gm paneer - cut into 1½" long pieces, 1" thick
4 tbsp besan (gram flour)
1 tsp salt
4 tbsp oil

GRIND TO A FINE PASTE (CHUTNEY)
1 cup fresh green dhania (green coriander)
1 green chilli
2 tsp saunf (fennel)
5-6 flakes garlic
1" piece ginger
4 tbsp lemon juice
½ tsp salt

1. Grind together dhania, green chilli, saunf, ginger, garlic, lemon juice and salt to a fine paste.
2. Slit the paneer pieces and keep aside.
3. Divide the chutney into 2 parts.
4. With one part of the chutney, stuff some chutney in the slits of all the paneer pieces. Keep the stuffed paneer aside.
5. Mix together the left over chutney, besan, salt and 4 tbsp oil. Rub this all over the stuffed paneer pieces.
6. Rub some oil generously over the grill of the oven or wire rack of a gas tandoor. Place paneer on the greased wire rack or grill of the oven.
7. Heat an oven to 180°C or a gas tandoor on moderate flame. Grill paneer for 15 minutes. Spoon some drops of oil or melted butter on the paneer pieces in the oven or tandoor and grill further for 5 minutes. Serve hot.

Note:
- To cook the tikkas in the oven, place a drip tray under the wire rack on which the tikkas are placed, to collect the drippings.
- While skewering or placing the tikka the pieces should be arranged such that there is atleast 1" gap between them so that each piece can get it's own space and heat all around to get cooked properly.
- When skewering delicate vegetables, it is advisable to use thinner skewers, then there is less chance of the vegetable break.

Matar Makhane ke Kebab

Delicious crunchy green kebabs. Very appetizing to look at!

Makes 8 kebabs

1 cup boiled or frozen shelled peas
1 cup makhanas (puffed lotus seeds)
1 tbsp oil
2 green chillies - chopped
2-3 tbsp cashewnuts
¾ tsp salt or to taste, ½ tsp pepper, ¼ tsp garam masala
seeds of 4-5 chhoti illaichi (green cardamoms)

1. Heat 1 tbsp oil in kadhai. Add makhanas and saute for 3-4 minutes.
2. Add cashewnuts and saute till cashews start changing colour. Remove makhanas and cashewnuts from the kadhai.
3. In the same kadhai (without any oil leftover), add peas and saute for 2 minutes. Remove peas from kadhai.
4. Grind makhanas and cashewnuts together to a rough powder.
5. Grind peas with green chillies to a fine paste.
6. Mix makhanas and pea paste. Add salt, pepper, garam masala and chhoti illaichi.
7. Makes small balls and flatten them to get small round kebabs (tikkis).
8. Shallow fry on tawa or pan in 1-2 tbsp oil till brown and crisp.
9. Sprinkle chaat masala and serve hot with chilli garlic chutney (see page- 119) and peanut cabbage relish (see page- 121).

Special Shami Kebab

Serves 4

½ cup kale chane (black gram)
1 tbsp chane ki dal (bengal gram split)
1 onion - very finely chopped
1 tsp oil
1 tsp ginger paste, ½ tsp garlic paste
2 slices bread - grind in a mixer to get fresh crumbs
salt to taste
¼ tsp amchoor (dried mango powder)

GRIND TOGETHER TO A COARSE POWDER
¼ tsp jeera, 1" stick dalchini
3-4 laung (cloves)
3-4 saboot kali mirch (peppercorns), seeds of 2 moti illaichi
1 dry, red chilli

FILLING
2 tbsp finely chopped mint (poodina), 4 tbsp grated mozzarella cheese

1. Soak kale channe with channe ki dal overnight or for 6-8 hours in water.
2. Put kale channe, channe ki dal, onion and oil in a pressure cooker. Add powdered spices and 1½ cups water also. Pressure cook to give 1 whistle. After the first whistle, keep on slow fire for 20 minutes. Remove from fire and let the pressure drop by itself.
3. If there is extra water, dry the channas for sometime on fire. There should just be a little water, enough to grind the channas to a fine paste.
4. Grind to a fine paste.
5. Remove channa mixture to a bowl. Add ginger-garlic paste, bread, salt and amchoor to taste.
6. Mix all ingredients of the filling together.
7. Make a small ball of the paste. Flatten it, put 1 tsp of filling. Press the filling. Pick up the sides and make a ball again. Flatten it slightly.
8. Shallow fry 4-5 pieces on a tawa in 3-4 tbsp oil on medium flame.
9. Serve with poodina chutney and garnished papad (see page 126).

Note: If the kebabs break on frying, roll in dry maida alone or in egg white first and then in maida. Fry on moderate heat.

Tandoori Phool

A good meal time side dish.

Serves 4-6

1 medium size gobi (cauliflower) - wash and keep whole with 1-2" stalk

MARINADE
¾ cup thick curd - hang for ½ hour
¼ cup thick cream or malai
1 tbsp oil
2 tbsp besan - roasted on a tawa for 1 minute or till fragrant
½ tbsp ginger paste
2 tsp tandoori masala
4-6 saboot kali mirch (black peppercorns) - crushed
½ tsp red chilli powder
¼ tsp haldi
1 tsp salt

TO SERVE
2 onions - cut into fine rings
2 tbsp finely chopped coriander
½ tsp chaat masala
1 tomato - cut into slices

1. Boil 4 cups water with 1 tsp salt.
2. Add cauliflower. When the water starts to boil again, remove from fire. Let the cauliflower be in hot water for 3-4 minutes. Remove from water and keep aside.
3. Wipe the cauliflower with a clean kitchen towel. Keep aside.
4. Mix together in a bowl all ingredients of the marinade. Insert the marinade inside the cauliflower florets, from the bottom also. Rub the top of the flower with the left over marinade. Keep aside for atleast 1 hour.
5. Brush the grilling rack of the oven generously with oil. Place the marinated cauliflower on the greased grilling rack.
6. Grill in a hot oven at 200°C for 30 minutes or more till brown specs appear on the cauliflower. Keep aside till serving time.
7. To serve, cut the whole cauliflower into 4 big pieces right through the stalk. Cut each piece further into 2 pieces. Sprinkle chaat masala.
8. Add fresh coriander and chaat masala to the onions.
9. To serve, heat gobi in an oven or microwave till really hot. Arrange the pieces neatly in a serving platter. Sprinkle lemon juice. Garnish with onion rings, tomato slices, lemon wedges and mint sprigs.

Gulnar Seekh

Makes 15

1 cup saboot masoor ki dal
1" piece ginger
8-10 flakes garlic
1 green chilli - chopped
1 tsp jeera
1 tsp garam masala
1 tsp red chilli powder, ¼ tsp amchoor
½ cup mashed paneer
3 tbsp cornflour
1 tsp salt or to taste
1-2 tsp lemon juice
3 tbsp oil
2 tbsp each of finely chopped capsicum, onion and tomato (without pulp)

TO SERVE
2 onions - cut into rings
juice of 1 lemon
a few poodina leaves

1. Soak saboot masoor dal for 2 hours. Strain.
2. Grind dal, ginger, garlic, green chilli and jeera to a thick smooth paste using the minimum amount of water. Keep dal paste aside.
3. Heat 3 tbsp oil in a heavy bottomed kadhai. Add dal. Stir-fry for 4-5 minutes on low flame till dal is dry and does not stick to the bottom of the kadhai. Remove from fire.
4. Mix cornflour, paneer, salt, garam masala, red chilli powder and amchoor with the dal. Add lemon juice. Mix well. Keep aside.
5. Heat 3-4 tbsp oil on a tawa or a non-stick pan for shallow frying.
6. Grease a skewer. Spread a ball of dal paste to make a 2" long kebab of the dal paste over the skewer.
7. Stick finely chopped onion, capsicum and tomatoes (without pulp) on the kebab by pressing onions etc. with the palm on to the kebab. Gently pull out the skewer & shallow fry the seekh in medium hot oil to a light brown colour.
8. Serve on a bed of onion rings sprinkled with lemon juice and poodina leaves and garnished papad (see page 126).

Arbi Tandoori

Try this different way of preparing arbi for dinner tonight!

Serves 4

½ kg arbi (calocasia) - medium size

MARINADE
1 cup curd - hang in a muslin cloth for ½ hour
1 tbsp tandoori masala
1 tsp ginger paste
6-8 peppercorns - crushed
½ tsp ajwain(carom seeds)
a pinch of haldi
1 tbsp oil
½ tsp salt
1 tbsp besan(gramflour)

OTHER INGREDIENTS
3 tbsp oil
1 tsp crushed saboot dhania (coriander seeds)
4-5 onions - cut into rings
½ tsp garam masala, ¼ tsp salt, or to taste
1½ tsp amchoor (dried mango powder)
3-4 green chillies - slit lengthwise
½" piece ginger - shredded

1. Hang curd in a muslin cloth for ½ hour.
2. Boil arbi in salted water with ½ tsp of amchoor, till soft. Peel and flatten the pieces.
3. Mix tandoori masala, ginger paste and crushed saboot kali mirch to hung curd. Add ajwain, a pinch of haldi for colour and 1 tbsp oil. Add ½ tsp salt and besan.
4. Heat an oven to 180°C or a gas tandoor on moderate flame. Grease the wire rack well. Dip arbi pieces in the prepared curd and arrange on the rack.
5. Keep in a hot oven for ½ hour. Grill a tray beneath till the curd dries up and forms a coating and arbi turns brownish. Keep arbi aside.
6. Heat 3 tbsp oil. Add crushed saboot dhania. Wait till it turns golden. Add onions rings. Cook till onions turn light brown.
7. Add garam masala, amchoor and salt. Add the arbi.
8. Add the shredded ginger and green chillies. Mix well. Stir fry for 3-4 minutes.
9. Remove from fire. Serve hot with til chutney (see page 119) and garnished papad (See page 126).

Tandoori Chaat

Picture on facing page   *Serves 4*

2 capsicums - deseed & cut into 1½" pieces (preferably 1 green & 1 red capsicum)
200 gm paneer - cut into 1" cubes (8 pieces)
2 small onions - each cut into 4 pieces
4 fresh pineapple slices - each cut into 4 pieces (see note)
2 tomatoes - each cut into 4 pieces and pulp removed
1 tsp garam masala
2 tbsp lemon juice
1 tbsp tandoori masala or barbecue masala
2 tbsp oil
1 tsp salt, or to taste
1½ tsp chaat masala

1. Mix all the vegetables, pineapple and paneer in a bowl.
2. Sprinkle all the ingredients on them. Mix well.
3. Grease the grill or wire rack of the oven or tandoor and first place the paneer, pineapple and onions only on the grill rack. Grill for about 15 minutes, till the edges start to change colour.
4. After the paneer is almost done, put the capsicum and tomatoes also on the wire rack with the paneer etc. Grill for 10 minutes.
5. Remove from the oven straight to the serving plate. Sprinkle some chaat masala and lemon juice, if you like.

Note: If tinned pineapple is being used, grill it in the second batch with capsicum and tomatoes since it is already soft.

Bhutte Ke Seekh Kebabs : Recipe on page 84, Tandoori Chaat ➤

INDIAN BREADS

Paranthas, Nans & Rotis

Nan Badaami

Makes 6

2½ cups (250 gms) maida (plain flour)
½ cup hot milk
1 tsp baking powder
½ cup warm water (approx.)
½ tsp salt
6-8 badaam (almonds) - skinned & cut into long thin pieces (slivered)
1 tbsp kasoori methi

1. Heat milk and put it in a shallow bowl or a paraat. Add baking powder to the hot milk. Mix well and keep it aside for 1-2 minutes till it starts to bubble.
2. Sift maida and salt together. Add maida to the hot milk. Mix.
3. Knead to a dough with just enough warm water to get a dough of rolling consistency. Knead once again with wet hands till very smooth and elastic.
4. Keep covered with a damp cloth in a warm place for 3-4 hours.
5. Make 6-8 balls. Cover with a damp cloth and keep aside for 15 minutes.
6. Heat a gas tandoor for 10 minutes on fire.
7. Roll out each ball to an oblong shape. Spread ghee all over. Fold 1" from one side (lengthways), so as to overlap an inch of the nan. Press on the joint with the belan (rolling pin).
8. Sprinkle some blanched (skin removed by dipping in hot water) and chopped almonds and kasoori methi. Press with a rolling pin (belan) lightly. Pull one side of the nan to give it a pointed end like the shape of the nan.
9. Apply some water on the back side of the nan. Stick in a hot gas tandoor.
10. Cook till nan is ready. Spread butter on the ready nan and serve hot.

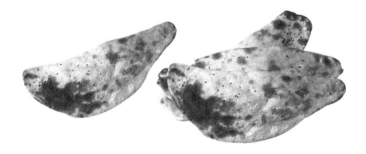

Lachha Parantha

Makes 6

2 cups atta (wheat flour), ½ tsp salt, 2 tbsp ghee
½ cup milk, ½ cup water

1. Sift flour and salt in a paraat (deep bowl). Rub in 1 tbsp ghee till the flour turns crumbly.
2. Mix water and milk together. Make a well in the middle of the flour. Pour milk-water mix gradually. Knead well to a dough of rolling consistency. Keep covered with a damp cloth for ½ hour.
3. Make 6 balls. Roll out each ball to a circle of 6" diameter. Spread some ghee all over. Sprinkle dry atta on half of the circle.
4. Fold into half to get a semi-circle. Spread ghee all over again. Put dry atta on half part of the semi-circle. Fold again lengthwise into half so that you get a long strip.
5. Apply ghee all over on the strip. Roll the strip from one end till the end, to form a flattened ball (pedha). Press gently. Roll out, applying very little pressure, to form the lachha parantha. If too much pressure is applied, the layers stick to each other and do not open up later.
6. Stick in a heated tandoor or shallow fry on a tawa. Place on a clean napkin and crush the parantha slightly, to open up the layers. Serve hot.

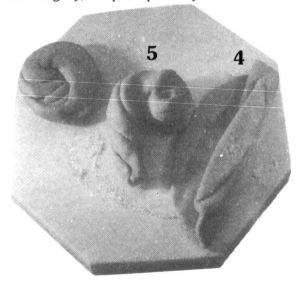

Poodina Parantha

Serves 4

KNEAD TOGETHER TO A DOUGH
2 cups atta (whole wheat flour)
2 tbsp poodina (mint leaves) - freshly chopped or dry
1 tsp ajwain (carom seeds)
2 tbsp ghee
½ tsp salt
½ tsp red chilli powder

TOPPING
2 tbsp dry poodina, 1 tsp ajwain
ghee or melted butter - enough to spread

1. Mix atta with all ingredients till crumbly. Add enough water to make a dough of rolling consistency. Cover and keep the dough aside for 30 minutes.
2. Make walnut sized balls. Roll out a little to make a thick chappati.
3. Spread 1 tsp melted butter or ghee all over. Roll to get a long strip of dough.
4. Coil the strip to get a flattened ball.
5. Roll out a little with the rolling pin (belan), applying no pressure at all, otherwise the layers do not open.
6. Sprinkle some dry poodina and a little ajwain. Press with the belan (rolling pin).
7. Stick in a heated tandoor or shallow fry on a tawa by frying on both sides with ghee till crisp and well browned.
8. Apply melted butter if made in the tandoor and crush slightly by placing on a clean napkin and serve.

Jeera Parantha

Makes 8

2 cups atta (whole wheat flour)
1 tbsp roasted jeera (bhuna jeera)
½ tsp ajwain (carom seeds)
2 tbsp ghee
½ tsp salt, ½ tsp red chilli powder

1. Mix atta with ajwain, 1 tbsp ghee, salt , chilli powder, and ½ of the jeera (½ tbsp). Add enough water to make a dough of rolling consistency. Cover and keep the dough aside for 30 minutes.
2. Make walnut sized balls. Roll out a little to make a thick chappati.
3. Spread 1 tsp ghee all over. Fold a little from the left and then right to meet in the centre. Fold the top and the bottom to now get a square.
4. Roll out to get a square parantha, but do not make it too thin. Sprinkle little bhuna jeera. Press with the belan (rolling pin).
5. Cook on a tawa, frying on both sides till crisp and well browned.

Tandoori Roti

Makes 6-7

2 ½ cups atta (whole wheat flour), ½ tsp salt
1 cup water (approx.)

PASTE TO SPREAD
2 tbsp ghee or oil mixed with 1 tbsp maida

1. Make a soft dough with atta, salt and water. Keep aside for half an hour.
2. Divide the dough into 6 equal balls. Flatten each ball, roll out each into a round of 5" diameter.
3. Spread some ghee mixed with maida.
4. Make a slit, starting from any one end till almost to the other end, leaving just 1".
5. Start rolling from the slit, to form an even cone.
6. Keeping the cone upright, press slightly to get a flattened, coiled disc.
7. Roll out with a belan to a diameter of 5", applying pressure only at the centre and not on the sides. The layers do not open if pressure is applied on the sides. Cook in a hot tandoor till brown specs appear.

Roomali Roti

Makes 12   *Picture on page 117*

DOUGH
1½ cups maida (plain flour)
1 cup atta
2 tbsp oil
½ tsp salt

PASTE
2 tbsp ghee
1 tbsp maida (plain flour)

1. Mix maida, atta, oil and salt with a little water to make a slightly stiff dough like the dough for puris. Keep aside covered with a damp cloth for 1 hour.
2. Make a paste of ghee and maida in a small bowl.
3. Make 2 lemon sized balls of the dough.
4. Roll out 1 ball to the size of a puri, about 5-6" diameter.
5. Spread 1 tsp of the ghee-maida paste on it. Keep aside in a plate.
6. Roll the second ball to the same size again and put this on the first roti spread with ghee.
7. Place the sandwiched rotis on the chakla and roll out together to a large thin roti using a little dry flour for rolling.
8. Heat a tawa on low heat and cook this roti on both sides very quickly. Do not make it brown.
9. Remove from fire and immediately separate the 2 rotis stuck by the paste.
10. Fold each roti into a triangle and keep soft in a casserole.

Missi Roti

Makes 10

1 cup besan (gram flour)
2 cups atta (wheat flour)
1 onion - very finely chopped
2 tbsp oil or melted ghee
¾ tsp salt
¾ tsp red chillies
2 pinches of haldi
1 tsp ajwain (carom seeds)
1 tsp anaardaana (pomegranate seeds) - whole or pounded
1 tbsp kasoori methi (dried fenugreek leaves)

1. Mix both flours. Add all other ingredients. Knead to a smooth dough of rolling consistency. Cover and keep aside for atleast 30 minutes.
2. Shape into 10 balls. Roll out each ball to a slightly thick, small chappati.
3. Cook it on hot tawa on both sides, when half done, roast on both sides on naked flame. Spread white butter or pure ghee on the hot roti. Serve.

Note: Missi roti cooks well in the tandoor also.
Missi roti is served with fresh butter and curd and mangoes in summer. Tomato or mango chutney goes well with it.

Keema Parantha

Serves 8

FILLING
250 gm keema (minced meat)
1 onion - chopped finely, 2 tsp ginger - chopped finely
3 tbsp oil
1 tsp dhania powder, ½ tsp garam masala, 1 tsp salt, ½ tsp red chilli powder
2 green chillies - chopped, 1 tbsp finely chopped fresh coriander

DOUGH
2 cups atta (wheat flour)
½ tsp salt, 1 tbsp ghee

TOPPING
1 tbsp kasoori methi (dry fenugreek leaves)

1. To prepare the dough, sift flour and salt. Rub in 1 tbsp ghee. Add enough water to make a dough. Keep aside for 30 minutes.
2. To prepare the filling, heat 3 tbsp oil and fry the chopped onion until rich brown. Add keema (mince) and ginger and mix well. Reduce heat. Add salt, dhania powder, red chilli powder and garam masala. Fry for 1-2 minutes. Cook covered on low heat for about 5 minutes, till the mince is cooked.
3. Add green chillies and 1 tbsp finely chopped coriander. If there is any water, uncover and dry the mince on fire. Keep the stuffing aside.
4. For tandoori parantha, (see note) divide the dough into 10 equal parts. Shape into round balls. Flatten each ball, roll out each into a round of 5" diameter. Spread 1 tsp full of ghee. Then spread 1-2 tbsp of filling all over.
5. Make a slit, starting from the centre till any one end. Start rolling from the slit, to form an even cone. Keeping the cone upright, press slightly.
6. Roll out, applying pressure only at the centre. Do not roll or press too much on the sides, otherwise the layers of parantha do not separate after cooking.
7. Sprinkle some kasoori methi and press with a rolling pin (belan).
8. Apply water on the back side of the parantha and stick carefully in a heated tandoor or place in a preheated oven in a greased tray.
9. Remove after a few minutes. Spread some ghee, serve hot.

Note: You can stuff the filling in an ordinary parantha and fry it on the tawa like any other bharwaan parantha. For bharwaan parantha roll out 2 small chappatis and sandwich them with keema filling. Press the sides well to seal the filling and roll out to a parantha.

CHUTNEYS
&
SALADS

Chicken Tikka : Recipe on page 24 ➢
Haryali Paneer Tikka : Recipe on page 100 ➢
Roomali Roti : Recipe on page 113 ➢

Dahi Poodina Chutney

Picture on page 1   *Serves 6*

GRIND TOGETHER
½ cup poodina (mint), ½ cup hara dhania (green coriander)
2 green chillies
½ onion, 2 flakes garlic
a pinch of kala namak, ¼ tsp bhuna jeera, salt to taste

ADD LATER
1½ cups curd - hang for 15 minutes
1 tsp oil

1. Wash coriander and mint leaves.
2. Grind coriander, mint, green chillies, onion and garlic with a little water to a paste.
3. Beat curd well till smooth.
4. To the hung curd, add the green paste, oil, kala namak, bhuna jeera and salt to taste. Serve with tandoori food.

Instant Khatti Mithi Chutney

Serves 6

1 tbsp amchoor (dried mango powder)
3 tbsp sugar or shakkar (gur)
½ tsp roasted jeera (cumin seeds)
¼ tsp red chilli powder
¼ tsp salt
¼ tsp garam masala
¼ cup water

1. Mix all ingredients together in a small heavy bottomed pan.
2. Cook on low flame, till all the ingredients dissolve properly and the chutney gets the right consistency. Remove from fire.

Chilli Garlic Chutney

Serves 8   *Picture on page 37*

l4-5 dry red chillies - deseeded and soaked in ¼ cup water
6-8 flakes garlic, 1 tsp saboot dhania, 1 tsp jeera, 1 tbsp oil
½ tsp salt, 1 tsp sugar
3 tbsp vinegar, ½ tsp soya sauce

1. For the chutney, grind the soaked chillies along with the water, garlic, dhania, jeera, oil and sugar and vinegar to a paste. Add soya sauce.

Til Chutney

Til is very popular in India. It has a distinctive flavour which goes well as a chutney.

Serves- 6   *Picture on page 47*

2 tbsp til (sesame seeds)
½ cup poodina (mint) leaves, 3 green chillies
1 large onion, 1 flake garlic
2½ tbsp tamarind (imli) pulp
¼ tsp salt or to taste

1. Roast til on a tawa (griddle). Keep 1 tbsp til aside.
2. Grind 1 tbsp roasted til with all the other ingredients in a grinder to a semi-liquid paste with little water if required.
3. Add 1 tbsp roasted til kept aside. Mix well. Serve.

Poodina Chutney

Serves 6

½ cup poodina leaves (½ bunch)
1 cup hara dhania (coriander) - chopped along with the stem
2 green chillies - chopped
1 onion - chopped
1½ tsp amchoor (dried mango powder)
1½ tsp sugar, ½ tsp salt

1. Wash coriander and mint leaves.
2. Grind all ingredients with just enough water to get the right chutney consistency.

Sirke Waale Pyaaz

Serves 4-6

12-13 small onions
½ cup white vinegar
½ cup water
1 tsp salt
½ tsp red chilli powder

1. Peel onions. Make a cross slit on each onion on the top.
2. Place in a bowl. Sprinkle salt and chilli powder on them and rub well.
3. Boil water and vinegar together in a pan. Remove from fire.
4. Pour the hot vinegar water over the onions in the bowl.
5. When the vinegar cools a little, transfer the onions and vinegar into a clean bottle. Keep in the refrigerator.
6. Use after a day.

Note: A few ginger match sticks and green chillies can also be added.

Khatti Arbi Salad

Serves 2-3

250 gm arbi (colocasia)
½ tsp salt, or to taste
¼ tsp red chilli powder
½ tsp chaat masala
1 green chilli - deseeded and chopped
2-3 tbsp chopped coriander
juice of 1 lemon

1. Boil and peel arbi. Cut into round slices of ¼" thickness.
2. Add salt, chilli powder and chaat masala. Mix lightly with a fork.
3. Add green chillies and coriander.
4. Sprinkle juice of ½ lemon. Toss well to mix. Use forks for mixing. Cover and keep aside till serving time.
5. At serving time sprinkle some more lemon juice and mix lightly. Serve at room temperature.

Peanut Cabbage Relish

Here is a totally different way of using peanuts. This relish goes well with almost all tandoori recipes.

Serves 6

6 tbsp roasted peanuts - crushed coarsely
1 small cabbage - chopped very finely
1 tbsp green coriander - minced
2 green chillies - minced
juice of 2 lemons, or to taste
2 tsp sugar
1 tsp salt, or to taste

1. Mix ½ tsp salt in the cabbage and set aside for 10 minutes to sweat.
2. Coarsely crush the peanuts on a chakla-belan (rolling board and pin).
3. Put peanuts in a bowl. Add all other ingredients except the cabbage.
4. Squeeze the cabbage. Mix well and serve.

Mixed Green Relish

This simple and uncomplicated preparation is as full of flavour as the fresh spring air.

Serves 4

1 capsicum
1 small onion - cut into rings and then cut the rings into 2 halves
1 cucumber
1 tbsp mint leaves - chopped
½ tsp black pepper powder
2 tbsp lemon juice
½ tsp salt, or to taste

1. Cut the capsicums into small, thin matchstick like pieces.
2. Remove the bitterness of the cucumber. Wash and cut it into thin slices lengthwise without peeling. Cut the slices into thin matchstick like pieces.
3. Put the greens and onions in cold water for 10 minutes to turn crisp.
4. Strain and leave in the strainer for 15 minutes. Wipe dry on a paper napkin.
5. Add the rest of the ingredients and serve.

ACCOMPANIMENTS

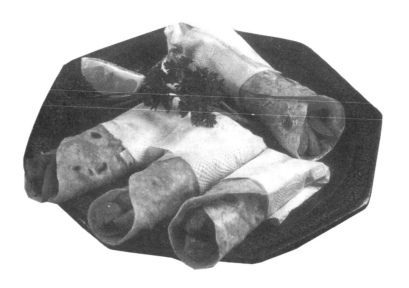

Dal Makhani

Picture on page 47   *Serves 6*

1 cup urad saboot (whole black beans)
2 tbsp channe ki dal (split gram dal)
1 tbsp ghee or oil
5 cups of water, 1½ tsp salt
3 tbsp ghee or oil
5 large tomatoes - pureed in a grinder
2 tsp dhania powder (coriander), ½ tsp garam masala
1 tbsp kasoori methi (dry fenugreek leaves)
2 tsp tomato ketchup
2-3 tbsp butter
½ cup milk
½ cup cream
a pinch of jaiphal (nutmeg)

GRIND TO A PASTE
2 dry whole red chillies, preferably Kashmiri red chillies - deseeded & soaked for
10 minutes and then drained
1" piece ginger
5-6 flakes garlic

1. Pressure cook both dals with 5 cups water, 1 tbsp ghee, salt and the ginger-garlic-chilli paste.
2. After the first whistle, keep on low flame for 40 minutes. Remove from fire. After the pressure drops, mash the hot dal a little. Keep aside.
3. Heat ghee. Add tomatoes pureed in a grinder. Cook until thick and dry.
4. Add the garam masala and coriander powder. Cook until ghee separates.
5. Add kasoori methi. Cook further for 1-2 minutes.
6. Add this tomato mixture to the boiled dal.
   Add tomato ketchup.
7. Add butter. Simmer on low flame for 20-25 minutes, stirring and mashing the dal occasionally with a karchhi against the sides of the cooker.
8. Add milk. Mix very well with a karcchi. Simmer for 15-20 minutes more, to get the right colour and smoothness.
9. Reduce heat. Add jaiphal. Mix. Add cream gradually, stirring continuously. Remove from fire. Serve.

Note: Originally the dal was cooked by leaving it overnight on the burning coal angithis. The longer the dal simmered, the better it tasted.

Paneer Makhani

Serves 4

250 gm paneer - cut into 1" cubes
5 large (500 gm) tomatoes - each cut into 4 pieces
2 tbsp desi ghee or butter and 2 tbsp oil
½ tsp jeera (cumin seeds)
4-5 flakes garlic and 1" piece ginger - ground to a paste (1½ tsp ginger-garlic paste)
1 tbsp kasoori methi (dried fenugreek leaves), 1 tsp tomato ketchup
2 tsp dhania powder, ½ tsp garam masala
1 tsp salt, or to taste, ½ tsp red chilli powder, preferably degi mirch
½ cup water
½-1 cup milk, approx.
½ cup cream (optional)

CASHEW PASTE
3 tbsp cashewnuts - soaked in ¼ cup warm water for 15 minutes and ground to a very fine paste

1. Boil tomatoes in ½ cup water. Simmer for 4-5 minutes on low heat till tomatoes turn soft. Remove from fire and cool. Grind the tomatoes along with the water to a smooth puree.
2. Heat oil and ghee or butter in a kadhai. Reduce heat. Add jeera. When it turns golden, add ginger-garlic paste.
3. When paste starts to change colour add the above tomato puree and cook till absolutely dry.
4. Add kasoori methi and tomato ketchup.
5. Add masalas - dhania powder, garam masala, salt and red chilli powder. Mix well for a few seconds. Cook till oil separates.
6. Add cashew paste. Mix well for 2 minutes.
7. Add water. Boil. Simmer on low heat for 4-5 minutes. Reduce heat.
8. Add the paneer cubes. Keep aside to cool till serving time.
9. At serving time, add enough milk to the cold paneer masala to get a thick curry, mix gently. (Remember to add milk only after the masala turns cold, to prevent the milk from curdling. After adding milk, heat curry on low heat.)
10. Heat on low heat, stirring continuously till just about to boil.
11. Add cream, keeping the heat very low and stirring continuously. Remove from fire immediately.
12. Garnish with 1 tbsp fresh cream, slit green chillies and coriander.

Chicken Tikka Kaathi Roti

Serves 6

DOUGH FOR ROTIS
250 gm (2½ cups) maida (plain flour)
½ tsp baking powder, 2 tbsp oil, 1 tsp salt or to taste,
¼ cup milk mixed with ½ cup water apporx.

FILLING
500 gm boneless cooked chicken tikka (prepare chicken tikka as given on page 24)
3 tbsp oil
1 large onion - ground to a paste
1 tbsp ginger-garlic paste
1 large tomato - chopped
red chilli powder and salt to taste
2 eggs - beaten
juice of 1 lemon
2 onions - thinly sliced & mixed with some hari chutney

1. To prepare the dough, sift maida with salt and baking powder. Add oil. Mix well. Knead with water and milk mixture into dough of rolling consistency. Keep aside covered for half an hour.
2. To prepare the filling, prepare chicken tikka as given on page 24.
3. Heat oil. Add onion paste and cook till light brown.
4. Add ginger-garlic paste and cook for 1 minute.
5. Add tomato and cook till tomato turns soft.
6. Add the cooked chicken tikka. Cover and cook on low flame till chicken turns tender and dry. Remove from fire and keep aside.
7. Squeeze lemon juice to taste and add a little salt and chilli powder to taste.
8. Mix sliced onions with pudina chutney. Keep aside.
9. Beat eggs and add a pinch of salt and pepper. Keep aside.
10. To prepare rotis, make chappatis of the prepared dough by cooking rotis lightly on both sides on a tawa. Keep cooked rotis in a casserole, to keep them soft.
11. At serving time, heat tawa. Add 1 tsp of oil and fry the chappati on one side only. Do not turn.
12. Pour 2 tbsp of beaten egg on the chappati and flip (turn) the roti to cook the egg. Remove from tawa, keeping the egg coated side up.
13. Sprinkle 1 tsp lemon juice on the egg coated side of the roti.
14. Arrange chicken tikka filling on one end of the roti. Sprinkle some onions on the chicken filling and roll the roti forward tightly to form the Kaathi Roti.
15. To serve, wrap the lower part of the rotis in a paper napkin and serve with dahi poodina chutney.

Garnished Pappad

Serves 12

**15 mini papads
1 onion - chopped, 2-3 green chillies - chopped
2 tbsp chopped coriander
1 tbsp butter or oil
2 tbsp freshly grated coconut (optional)
1 tomato - deseeded and cut into tiny pieces (diced)
¼ tsp red chilli powder
½ tsp salt or to taste, ¼ tsp pepper**

1. Heat 1 tbsp butter or oil.
2. Add onion and green chillies. Cook till soft. Add chopped fresh coriander, red chilli powder, salt, pepper and freshly shredded coconut. Mix well. Cook for 3-4 minutes. Add tomatoes. Mix and remove from fire.
3. Roast or fry the mini papads.
4. Spread spoon full of the mixture on each papad.
5. Sprinkle generously with chaat masala and serve with poodina chutney (see page 119).

Mixed Vegetable Raita

Servings 4-5

**2½ cups (½ kg) curd
1 onion - chopped finely
1 tomato - chopped finely
2 green chillies - chopped finely
½ carrot - grated
½ kheera (cucumber)- grated
a pinch of powdered sugar, ¾ tsp bhuna jeera (roasted cumin)
salt, black pepper to taste
1 tbsp of chopped coriander**

1. Beat curd till smooth.
2. Add all ingredients to the curd. Serve cold.

Lamb Tikka Masala : Recipe on page 53 ➤
Achari Paneer Tikka : Recipe on page 82 ➤

Nita Mehta's BEST SELLERS

Delicious Parlour ICE CREAMS

DESSERTS & PUDDINGS

CAKES & CHOCOLATES

Food for Children

BREAKFAST Veg. Special

The Art of BAKING

JHATPAT KHAANA

Indian Cooking Handi Tawa Kadhai

The Best of CHICKEN Recipes

Different ways with CHAAWAL

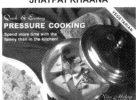
PRESSURE COOKING

Dal & Roti

PARTY FOOD

STAY SLIM...EAT RIGHT

LOW FAT Tasty Recipes

LOSE WEIGHT

PASTA & CORN

SOUTH INDIAN Favourites

Taste of GUJARAT

Mocktails & Snacks

NAVRATRI RECIPES

Green Vegetables

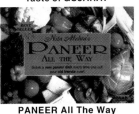
PANEER All The Way

MORE PANEER

Eggless OVEN Recipes

BREAKFAST Non-Vegetarian

Favourite Non-Veg Dishes

CHINESE Non-Vegetarian

NEW RELEASES BY Nita Mehta

The Best of
NON-VEGETARIAN

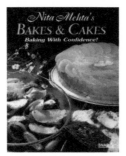

BAKES & CAKES
Baking with Confidence!

The Best of
CHICKEN & PANEER

QUICK
Vegetarian Cooking

MUGHLAI Khaana

(AWARD WINNER)

INDIAN VEGETARIAN Cookbook

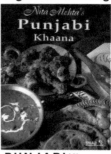

PUNJABI Khaana

Flavours of INDIAN COOKING
(All Colour)

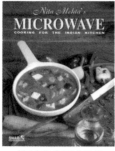

MICROWAVE
cooking for the Indian kitchen

Tempting SNACKS

ITALIAN
cooking for the Indian kitchen

CONTINENTAL
cooking for the Indian kitchen

CHINESE
cooking for the Indian kitchen

LOW CALORIE
cooking for the Indian kitchen

OVEN Recipe–NonVeg.

Vegetarian Wonders

Perfect Vegetarian cookery

The Best of MUTTON